Guide to State Parks of the
Sonoma Coast
and Russian River

Guide to State Parks of the
Sonoma Coast
and Russian River

Stephen W. Hinch

 **ANNADEL
PRESS**
Santa Rosa, California

Printed in the United States of America
First Printing, May 1998

Library of Congress Catalog Card Number: 98-70095
ISBN 0-9661999-2-8

Unless otherwise indicated, all photographs, maps, and line drawings are by the author.

Cover: purple bush lupine and Indian paintbrush bloom above Furlong Gulch, Sonoma Coast State Beach.

Warning. Information in this book is correct to the best of the author's knowledge at the time of publication. Author and publisher assume no liability for damages arising from errors, omissions, or misleading information in this guide, regardless of cause. You must always take responsibility for your own health and safety. Before hiking, always study maps carefully. Signposts are easily defaced or removed, so never depend only on them for guidance. Safety and conditions of trails, beaches, and tidepools change regularly, so always check with rangers for current conditions of unfamiliar areas.

A portion of the profits from the sale of this book are donated to the Stewards of Slavianka, the volunteer association that works in cooperation with the California Department of Parks and Recreation to provide interpretive programs and maintenance for parks in the Russian River/Mendocino District.

Annadel Press, P.O. Box 9398, Santa Rosa, CA 95405

To my family: Nicki, Greg, and Juliana

Stewards of Slavianka

"Slavianka" was the name given to the Russian River by 19th century Russian settlers at Fort Ross. It means "little Slavic girl." Stewards of Slavianka (SOS) is the nonprofit volunteer interpretive association that works in cooperation with the California Department of Parks and Recreation in the Russian River/Mendocino District. SOS volunteers conduct Whale Watch, Seal Watch, Junior Ranger and Campfire programs, staff visitors' centers and lead nature walks at Salt Point, Sonoma Coast, Armstrong Redwoods, and Austin Creek. SOS receives no state money and is primarily supported through sale of interpretive items in the visitor's centers, the sale of firewood at State Park campgrounds, memberships, and donations. Members receive a quarterly newsletter with information about the District's parks, special events for members, and opportunities for volunteering. Members are also entitled to discounts on purchases at visitor's centers and may earn annual day-use passes. To join SOS, write the Stewards of Slavianka at P.O. Box 221, Duncans Mills, CA 95430, call 707-869-9177, or e-mail at sos@wco.com. Also visit the SOS Internet home page at:

http://www.parks.sonoma.net/SOS.html

Fort Ross Interpretive Association

The Fort Ross Interpretive Association was formed to promote the educational and interpretive activities of Fort Ross State Historic Park. Fort Ross Interpretive Association is dedicated to the protection of the natural setting and to the preservation of an interpretation of the flow of history at Fort Ross: Indian, Russian, and Ranch. The association supports the park library, interpretive displays, archeological and ethnographic research, restoration of buildings, maintenance of the old Russian orchard, and internships for Russian and American scholars. Special events include Living History Day, recreating a typical day in the Russian period, and Ranch Day, celebrating life as it may have been in the late 1800's during the Call family period. To join the Fort Ross Interpretive Association, write to the association at 19005 Coast Highway One, Jenner, CA 95450, call 707-847-3437, or e-mail at fria@mcn.org. Also visit their Internet home page at:

http:\\www.mcn.org/1/rrparks/fria/fria.htm

Acknowledgements

Though I had explored the parks of the Sonoma Coast and Russian River area for over twenty years when I set out to write this book, I would hardly have considered myself an expert on them! Without the help of a great many people I could never have completed such an ambitious task.

First, no project of this magnitude would have been possible without support on the home front. Thanks go to my wife, Nicki, who not only tolerated my long hours in front of the computer but also proofread the entire manuscript. My son, Greg, and daughter, Juliana also endured the times I dragged them along to explore an overgrown trail or isolated beach.

I would also like to recognize the continual support and encouragement I received from the Stewards of Slavianka. Carrie Browder gave much encouragement and proof-read portions of the book. Michele Luna and Ruby Herrick were ardent supporters and helped me acquire some of the photographs. Joyce Bacci provided valuable insights into the history of her former home, Austin Creek State Recreation Area. Bob Wale furnished several excellent photographs. Bea Brunn and Frank Huntley taught me much about the natural history of gray whales. I also thank SOS president Lanny Keyston and the entire SOS board for supporting my efforts.

From the Parks Department, I would like to recognize a number of people for providing valuable information and reviewing the chapters. From Sonoma Coast State Beach I thank Crystal Matthews, Rich Lawton, and Rex Grady; from Fort Ross, Dan Murley, Bill Walton, and Sarah Gould-Ginesi; from Salt Point, Karen Broderick; and from Armstrong Redwoods/Austin Creek, Chazz Potthast. I would also like to thank District Interpretive Specialist Rick Royer and District Superintendent Bob LaBelle for their ongoing support.

Finally, I would like to give special recognition to Russ Whitman, the Stewards of Slavianka volunteer who originally drew me into SOS activities and whose gentle encouragement has guided me through this and other SOS projects. He also provided many excellent photographs of Armstrong Redwoods and Austin Creek.

A solitary figure explores an isolated beach at Bodega Head.

Contents

After a winter storm, driftwood litters the mouth of the Russian River.

Strange, honeycomb-shaped tafoni sandstone is common at Salt Point State Park.

Introduction to the Sonoma Coast

An hour's drive north of San Francisco you'll find one of the most spectacular sections of Pacific shoreline in all of California. Stretching from Bodega Bay to Gualala Point, the Sonoma Coast extends across sixty miles of windswept cliffs, isolated beaches, and crashing surf. Painters, photographers, and poets have all been inspired by Sonoma County's shores. Countless others have come to explore a surging tidepool or bask in the glow of a red Pacific sunset.

Four state parks help protect the natural beauty and historical significance of this magnificent coast, and two more lie a dozen miles inland. Sonoma Coast State Beach, Fort Ross State Historic Park, Salt Point State Park, Kruse Rhododendron State Reserve, Armstrong Redwoods State Reserve, and Austin Creek State Recreation Area are all easily accessible and open to a wide range of pursuits.

Each park has a distinctive character. Sonoma Coast State Beach is a geological wonder and popular escape from summer heat. At Fort Ross, the emphasis is on the history of a restored Russian stockade. Outdoor activities such as abalone diving, fishing, and hiking are the primary draw at Salt Point, while colorful rhododendron blooms bring throngs of visitors to Kruse Rhododendron State Reserve each spring. Armstrong Redwoods protects the last major stand of old-growth redwoods in Sonoma County, and nearby Austin Creek offers panoramic views from its oak-covered hillsides.

The Sonoma Coast is a region of great geologic activity. Even the casual observer will notice the rugged nature of the shore, but if you really get out and explore, you'll find much more evidence of upheaval. In the hills above the coast, great rifts scar the earth. Elongated ponds of water stand incongruously atop ridges where no streams can fill them. Fences and roads jog abruptly, as if built by separate groups who couldn't agree on where to meet. To really understand this coast, we first need a brief lesson in geology.

A Land in Upheaval

Take a map of Sonoma County and study the shape of its coast. Start in the south at Bodega Head, a finger of land that juts into the sea at the north-

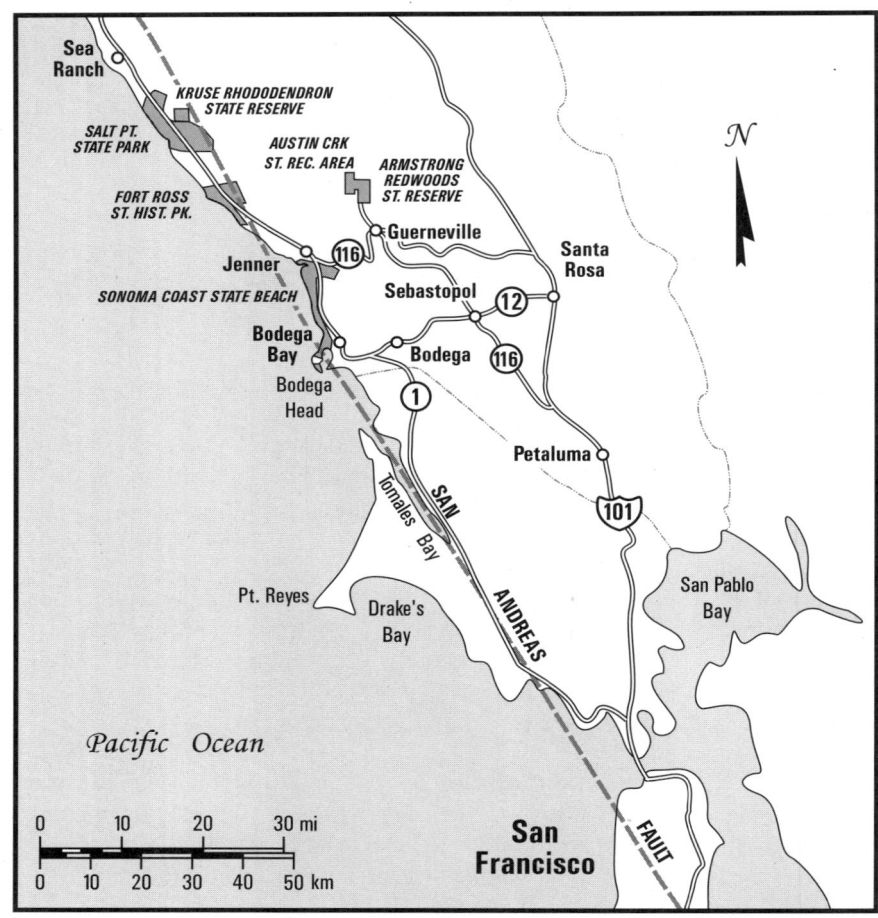

Map of Sonoma Coast region.

ern end of Bodega Bay. From here, follow the coastline south to Tomales Bay, a long, narrow inlet in Marin County that looks like, but isn't, the mouth of a large river.

Now take a ruler, draw a line through the middle of Tomales Bay, and continue northwestward into Sonoma County. The line will cut across Bodega Head, then run out to sea before making landfall again just south of Fort Ross. From there it will follow the South Fork of the Gualala River all the way into Mendocino County.

The line you have drawn is the great San Andreas Fault. Stretching for 700 miles from Southern California to the Mendocino Coast, the San Andreas is perhaps the most famous region of earthquake activity in the entire world. It was here near Tomales Bay (actually a fault valley long ago

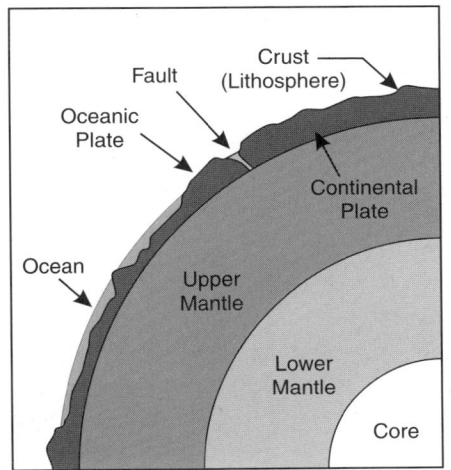

Cross section of the earth. Continental plates that form the earth's crust ride along the mantle. Earthquakes occur when two adjacent plates abruptly move past one another.

flooded by the sea) where the earth ruptured to cause the great San Francisco earthquake of 1906. The fault moved again in 1989 near San Jose, causing the famous Loma Prieta earthquake that collapsed freeways and broke a section of the San Francisco Bay Bridge.

The San Andreas Fault is an important geologic feature throughout the Bay Area. It lies at the interface of two massive continental plates: the Pacific Plate to the west and the North American Plate to the east. As these two plates collide, pressure builds at the interface until, in a sudden release of energy we call an earthquake, the two plates slip past each other to relieve the stress.

Over the last 30 million years, the Pacific Plate has moved hundreds of miles northward. We know this because rocks west of the fault near San Francisco match similar formations on the east side 300 miles to the south. On average, the relative motion between the plates is about 2 to 4 inches

This sag pond in the hills above Fort Ross was formed when the ground sank along the San Andreas fault.

Hundreds of thousands of years ago the rock formation on the right was a sea stack in the ocean. As this land near Shell Beach rose, it was left high and dry. The same fate may eventually await Gull Rock, a modern sea stack on the left.

per year. Sometimes, though, the movement is much greater. During the 1906 earthquake, a section of the fault in Point Reyes moved as much as 21 feet in just a few minutes!

The rugged profile of the Sonoma Coast is the result of constant erosion by water and wind. Seaside cliffs regularly crumble into the sea, leaving the surf littered with half-submerged rocky outcroppings. The largest of these are called sea stacks. Sonoma cliffs are notoriously unstable. Despite numerous posted warning signs, people are killed or injured every year in falls from cliff edges.

The Pacific Plate is rising as it moves northwestward. At various points along the coast, sea stacks that once lay in the ocean now rest on dry land a hundred feet higher. Two excellent examples are visible on Sonoma Coast State Beach just north of Shell Beach.

Early History of the Coast

Over the years, more nations have laid claims to Sonoma County than anywhere else in the United States. Before the Stars and Stripes, the flags of England, Russia, Spain, Mexico, and the California Republic all flew over this coast.

The first inhabitants, though, didn't carry a flag. For at least seven thousand years this land was the domain of Native Americans. At the time of European contact, it was split between two major Indian cultures. The Coast

Miwok lived from about the Russian River south to the Golden Gate, while the Pomo lived north of the river on into Mendocino County.

Though they sometimes bartered with each other, the two cultures evolved separately and spoke vastly different languages. Unlike their brethren on the great plains, neither the Miwok nor the Pomo were nomadic tribesmen. Amid such fertile surroundings there was little need to migrate in search of food. They lived instead in small tribelets with well-defined boundaries. They were renown for their exquisite basketmaking skills. The Pomo in particular carried the art of basketry to its highest levels in America.

João Rodrigues Cabrillo, a Portugese explorer under the command of the viceroy of New Spain, was the first European to intrude on this idyllic setting. In 1542 his expedition, searching for the mythical Northwest Passage, sighted land near the future site of Fort Ross. Though he was undoubtedly the first European to view the Sonoma Coast, Cabrillo died during the voyage and reports of his expedition were soon forgotten.

The first European to set foot on Sonoma County soil may well have been the English buccaneer Francis Drake. In the summer of 1579, after a year of plundering Spanish ships in the Pacific, he landed on the north coast to repair his leaking ship, *Golden Hind*. For five weeks, Drake and his men

Campbell Cove along the east side of Bodega Head may have been the site of Francis Drake's landing in 1579. The 12-story deep pond in the foreground is Hole-in-the-Head, the lone remnant of an ill-conceived 1960's nuclear power plant. (Photo by Bob Wale.)

explored the land. They befriended the local Indians, and when he left, Drake posted "a plate of brasse, fast nailed to a great and firme post," claiming the land for the Queen.

Unfortunately, Drake's logbook is lost in antiquity, so the precise spot of his landing is unknown. Every sandbar from San Diego to Eureka has at one time or another claimed him as its own. Two of the most likely spots are Bodega Bay and Drake's Bay. (A minority opinion favoring San Francisco Bay seems based on little more than wishful thinking.) Though many scholars favor Drake's Bay, Bodega Bay more closely matches the historical record. It is also the better harbor, a fact not likely to be lost on an experienced seaman like Drake.

After Drake, Europeans virtually ignored California for 200 years. In 1775, the Spanish explorer Juan de la Bodega y Quadra landed briefly at Bodega Bay and thereby conferred its name. Not until Russian settlement in the early 1800's, however, did the Sonoma Coast become of serious interest to Europeans. The Russians desperately needed a steady supply of fruits and vegetables for their Alaskan seal-hunting colonies. Aleksandr Baranov, manager of these colonies, sent expeditions south to hunt sea otters and scout sites for an agricultural colony along the coast north of San Francisco. Ivan Kuskov built a temporary site at Bodega Bay in 1809, then returned in 1812 to found a permanent settlement at Fort Ross. Though the Spanish at San Francisco protested loudly, they were never strong enough to attempt a forcible eviction. In fact, San Francisco was such a remote outpost that the locals tended to ignore the protestations emanating from colonial headquarters in faraway Mexico. Surreptitious trading was common, and Spanish officials were even occasionally invited to celebrations at the fort.

The Russians occupied Fort Ross for nearly thirty years, never firing a shot in anger. It never lived up to its agricultural promise, but the harvest of sea otter furs was initially profitable. By the 1830's, though, the otters had

You can still see occasional remnants of the old narrow-gauge railroad that once ran from Sausalito to Cazadero. These timbers were part of a trestle near Valley Ford.

A Graveyard of Ships

Over the years, the rugged shores of Sonoma County have contributed to more than their share of ship disasters. Frequent fogs, rough seas, and a rocky coastline create treacherous conditions for unwary seamen. The latter half of the nineteenth century was a particularly deadly time. In these days before automobiles and paved highways, ocean travel was the routine method of transportation for both passengers and cargoes along the coast. With only the most rudimentary navigational equipment, courageous captains regularly put their small schooners into doghole ports under extremely difficult conditions.

The annals are full of stories of Sonoma County shipwrecks. In many cases only terse accounts remain, revealing little of the terrors for those unlucky souls involved: "*Ellen H. Wood*, brig, wrecked at Salt Point, 1859, 4 dead; *Hannah Louise*, schooner, capsized at Russian Gulch, 1872, 1 dead; *Liberty*, schooner, wrecked at Timber Cove, 1872, 1 dead; *Mary D. Pomeroy*, schooner, capsized in a gale and washed ashore at Salt Point, 1879, 15 missing; *Two Brothers*, schooner, capsized at Bodega Head, 1883, 4 dead; *Volunteer*, 4-masted schooner, wrecked at Bodega Head, 1906, 3 dead, including captain's two children, when his wife ordered their lifeboat into the dangerous surf instead of open sea."

Sometimes, the stories have happier endings. In 1908 the passenger steamship *Pomona* struck a submerged reef and foundered at Fort Ross. The Call family, owners of the ranch at Fort Ross, came down the bluff to help save the 84 passengers and crew.

Time has erased all evidence of most of these wrecks, but an occasional trace still remains. The 386-foot steamship freighter *Norlina*, built in 1909, ran aground at Gerstle Cove in heavy fog the night of August 4, 1926. Her rusted hulk still rests in shallow water south of the cove, visible at low tide to those who know where to look.

been nearly exterminated. Debts mounted year by year until the Russians finally withdrew. They sold the fort to John Sutter and abandoned California in 1841.

Mexico was alarmed at the Russian incursion. To prevent further foreign expansion they vowed to settle the north coast as quickly as possible. Throughout the 1830's and early 1840's, the government made numerous land grants to encourage settlement. In 1840 Stephen Smith received the 35,000-acre Bodega Rancho, stretching from the Russian River south to Estero Americano. The 61-year-old Yankee sea captain settled the land with his 16-year-old Peruvian bride, Manuella. Further north, German immigrants Charles Meyer and Ernest Rufus in 1846 received the 18,000-acre German Rancho covering the coast from Salt Point to Gualala. Between these two lay the massive Muniz Rancho, awarded to Manuel Torres in 1845.

The rancho period in Sonoma County was destined to be brief. The era of American westward migration had begun, and the newcomers resented a system that locked them out of land ownership. The Bear Flag Revolt of 1846 began in the nearby town of Sonoma, and for 25 days in June and July of that year, California existed as an independent republic. Even after the United States annexed the territory and proclaimed the land grants to be

In the late 1800's, small lumber schooners were loaded by way of precarious affairs known as slide chutes. (Photo courtesy of Salt Point State Park.)

valid, the newcomers ignored them. Most grants were eventually sold off piecemeal by owners unwilling to endure years of protracted legal battles and occasional gunplay over squatters on their lands.

Starting in the 1860's and lasting until a narrow-gauge railroad was put through to the Russian River in the late 1880's, the Sonoma Coast was a shipping center for timber from the nearby redwood forests. There were no real ports along this coast. Instead, lumber was loaded onto schooners from such tiny outports as Duncan's Landing, Fort Ross Cove, Timber Cove, and Stewart's Point. Captains of large vessels scornfully called them "doghole ports" because they were allegedly barely large enough for a dog to turn around. The small, two-masted lumber schooners were invariably piloted by seasoned Scandinavian captains used to maneuvering in the cramped confines of Norwegian fjords.

Schooners anchored in these outports were loaded by way of a precarious affair known as a slide chute—a wooden ramp supported by pillars that extended down from a high bluff to the ship's deck. Boards were individually launched down the ramp to the waiting hands of a crewman on deck. A series of brakes were supposed to slow the boards, but mishaps were common, especially in rough weather. The slide chute was used to load everything from lumber to supplies to the occasional intrepid passenger. If a storm came up, the schooner would have to put quickly to sea to avoid being dashed on the rocks.

In 1873, George W. Call purchased 15,000 acres around Fort Ross and established the Call Ranch. The site of the former Russian outpost was sold to the California Historical Landmarks Committee in 1903 and turned over to the State in 1906. Sonoma Coast State Beach was acquired in 1934 and Salt Point State Park in 1968.

Exploring the Coast

The main road linking the various communities along the Sonoma Coast is a winding, two-lane adventure called State Highway 1. Don't expect to get anywhere along it in a hurry. The combination of twisting hillside curves, drivers dazzled by the scenery, and the occasional bicyclist, pedestrian, or farm animal make it unsafe to hurry. Take it easy, plan a leisurely journey, and enjoy the drive. The road includes numerous turnouts that allow you to safely observe the spectacular views and let more impatient traffic pass.

There are two popular routes west to the coast from US 101. The southern route departs the freeway in Santa Rosa at the Highway 12 exit, heads west to Sebastopol, and continues along the Bodega Highway to Highway 1 just south of Bodega Bay. The northern route exits at River Road to Guerneville, then along Highway 116 to Highway 1 at Jenner. Both routes are especially scenic, and both can be heavily traveled, particularly on summer weekends.

Though it is possible to see the entire coast in a single day, a better choice is to plan at least two or three days. Numerous fine accommodations can be found all along the coast at places such as Bodega Bay, Jenner, Timber Cove, and Sea Ranch. For the more adventurous, several campgrounds suitable for tent or RV camping are located at Sonoma Coast, Fort Ross, and Salt Point State Parks, as well as in several county parks and private campgrounds. You may also choose to combine your visit with a tour of the exceptional Sonoma County wine country. (For touring recommendations, stop at the Sonoma County Wine and Visitors Center in Rohnert Park or call 707-586-3795.)

A typical coastal tour starts from Bodega Highway out of Sebastopol. The route winds through apple orchards and pasture lands to the town of Bodega (not to be confused with Bodega Bay), half a mile east of the Highway 1 junc-

Stewarts Point Store is typical of shops along the Sonoma Coast. (photo by Bob Wale.)

The town of Bodega Bay is home to the largest fishing fleet between San Francisco and Eureka.

tion. Captain Stephen Smith built California's first steam-powered saw mill here in the 1840's. The town is home to art galleries and antique shops along with several historic buildings. The most prominent is St. Teresa's Church, built in 1859 and the subject of a famous Ansel Adams photograph. Behind the church is Potter School House, featured in Alfred Hitchcock's classic 1963 thriller, *The Birds*. A historic cemetery west of town is the final resting place for many early area residents.

This region was originally settled by Russian pioneers in the early 1800's. They built the farming community of Kuskov along the present Salmon Creek Road to help supply their settlement at Fort Ross. No trace of Kuskov or its inhabitants remains today.

After leaving Bodega, turn right at the Highway 1 junction. The road winds four miles through Cheney Creek Canyon to Bodega Bay, centerpiece of the southern coast. Here you will find shops, markets, restaurants, and accommodations. Spud Point Marina on West Shore Road is home to a large fishing fleet. From December through April, wildlife enthusiasts converge on Bodega Head as a premier spot for whale watching. The University of California also operates a marine laboratory and refuge here. The entire Bodega Bay area is an important stopover for migratory birds and draws hordes of bird watchers during migration.

Doran Beach, at the southern end of the harbor, is the site of a county park and campground. The headquarters for Sonoma Coast State Beach are located at Salmon Creek Beach, just north of town. This long, sandy beach is a popular destination on hot summer weekends. For part of the winter, the cypress and eucalyptus groves adjacent to nearby Bodega Dunes are home to thousands of Monarch butterflies.

State beaches lie interspersed with private property all along the coast to Jenner. Portuguese Beach and Duncan's Cove are popular rock fishing and surf netting spots. Shell Beach is a frequent destination for school field trips to explore tidepool marine life. And a large seal colony is a fixture along the Russian River at the north end of Goat Rock Beach.

The town of Jenner sits above the mouth of the Russian River. Originally a lumber town, it is now home to a community of artists and fishermen. Until the highway bridge was built in the 1930's, the only way across the river here was by ferry.

North of Jenner the highway quickly winds 600 feet above the sea. Known as Sonoma's Lost Coast, its shoreline is accessible only to the dedicated hiker. Come properly equipped and pay attention to tide tables if you want to explore this beautiful but isolated region.

Eleven miles north of Jenner lies Fort Ross, site of the first permanent settlement along the California coast north of San Francisco. The restored fort now stands as part of Fort Ross State Historic Park. There are also several miles of hiking trails within the park.

Just beyond Fort Ross is the town of Timber Cove, founded as a lumbering community in the late 1800's. It once was a main shipping point for cordwood, fence posts, tanbark, and railroad ties. A Timber Cove landmark is the famous Bufano peace statue, *The Expanding Universe*, at the Timber Cove Inn. The internationally acclaimed artist and pacifist Benjamin Bufano erected the sculpture in 1965 as a monument to the folly of war.

Six-thousand-acre Salt Point State Park lies north of Timber Cove. Its varied terrain includes forested mountains, a sandy ocean cove, and sculptured rocky promontories. Salt Point is a popular site for abalone diving, as well as camping, hiking, picnicking, and horseback riding. Directly adjacent is Kruse Rhododendron State Reserve, donated to the state by Edward P.E. Kruse in 1933. The trails through this park are especially picturesque when the rhododendrons bloom in May.

Near the northern end of the county lies a planned community, The Sea Ranch. The town was founded in the mid-1960's and includes a golf course,

Highway 1 between Jenner and Fort Ross is a winding, two-lane road that climbs as high as 600 feet above the sea.

California State Park System
General Rules and Regulations

The following rules and regulations apply to all units of the California State Park System. These rules protect park areas for the enjoyment of future generations as well as for the convenience and safety of the park visitors. In addition to these general rules, refer to supplemental rules for individual parks in their respective chapters.

Plant and animal life. All plants and animals within the parks are protected and must not be disturbed.

Camping. Camping is permitted only in designated campsites. Campsite use must be paid for in advance. Many developed campgrounds may be reserved by phone through the reservation service for California State Parks. Sites may be reserved up to 8 weeks in advance and as late as two days prior to arrival by calling toll-free at 800-444-7275, 8:00 am to 5:00 pm Pacific Time, 7 days a week. There is a fee for cancellations. To hold a campsite, it must be reserved or occupied. To prevent encroachment on others, the limits of each campsite may be regulated by the District Superintendent.

Hunting. Hunting is not allowed in units of the State Park System. Possession of loaded firearms and air rifles is prohibited. Exceptions are in recreation areas that have been designated by the State Park and Recreation Commission (none of the parks in the Sonoma Coast/Russian River region have been so designated).

Collecting. All living and non-living things are protected and may not be collected. You must obtain a permit from the district superintendent for any exceptions. Decaying vegetation forms humus and assists the growth of live trees and other plants. For this reason the gathering of down wood is prohibited. Fuel is sold in the parks for your convenience. (When considered a hazard, down wood is converted to fuel by park personnel.) Refer to the supplemental rules for Sonoma Coast State Beach for rules regarding the collection of driftwood.

Fires. Fires are permitted only in facilities provided for this purpose. This is necessary to prevent disastrous wildfires. Portable stoves may be used in designated areas. It is the responsibility of every visitor to use extreme caution with any burning materials, including tobacco. All fireworks are prohibited.

Pets. Domestic animals, including dogs and cats, are not permitted to run at large in any unit of the State Park System. Dogs and cats must be in a tent or vehicle during nighttime hours. Dogs must be controlled on a leash no longer than six feet during the day. Proof of valid rabies innoculation or a valid license is required for all dogs. Dogs are prohibited on some beaches and other areas; refer to supplemental rules for each park.

Generators. Electric generators may be operated only between 8:00 am and 8:00 pm.

Vehicles. All vehicle travel must be confined to designated roads or areas. The speed limit for all vehicles is 15 miles per hour in camp, picnic, utility, and headquarters areas, and areas of general assemblage. In no event shall any vehicle be driven at a speed greater than 25 miles per hour in other areas unless otherwise posted. All vehicles and drivers must be licensed. Parking is permitted only in designated areas.

Refuse. Trash, including garbage, cigarettes, paper boxes, bottles, ashes, and other rubbish, shall be placed only in designated receptacles. Your pleasure and pride in your parks will be enhanced when they are kept clean.

lodge, and over 1000 upscale homes that have been designed to blend with the coastal landscape.

Climate

Mark Twain once said "the coldest winter I ever spent was one summer in San Francisco." The English buccaneer Francis Drake described the area as a land of "stynking fogges," and complained that despite landing in the height of summer, "were wee continually visited with like nipping colds." Clearly, the warm, sunny beaches of southern California are absent here, but despite the bad publicity, the Sonoma Coast is not as harsh as it might sound. The rainy season is mainly confined between the months of October and March. Winter temperatures rarely approach freezing, though with the frequent winds it often seems colder. Summers can actually be quite pleasant when the fog recedes. At these times, a trip to the coast can be a welcome respite from the hundred-plus degree temperatures inland.

Regardless of the time of year, come prepared for cool, windy weather. Bring a sweater or jacket and leave it in the car if you don't need it. In winter, additional apparel should include a hat, gloves, and water-repellent rain shell. Don't be fooled by warmer weather inland. Even a few miles from the coast the temperature can be 20 degrees F higher. At times, the town of Bodega Bay can be bathed in warm sunlight while across the sand dunes, Salmon Creek Beach and the northern coast can be fogged in. It is also wise to bring sunscreen or similar protection. Fog or clouds offer little shelter from harmful rays, so use it even on an overcast day.

The cold waters of the Sonoma Coast are not suitable for casual swimming. Strong waves and rip currents can make it dangerous even to play in the surf. Diehard surfers and skin divers should venture into the ocean only if they are in good physical condition, adequately trained, and properly equipped with wet suits. Never enter the water alone!

Animal Life

Land Mammals. Early travelers were quick to note the variety of wildlife inhabiting the Sonoma Coast. Kyrill Khlebnikov, a Russian who visited Fort Ross in the early 1800's, observed "bears, lynx, ordinary wolves, and the small ones which the Spaniards call coyotes." The most majestic and dangerous animal was the California grizzly bear. Hunted mercilessly, it was driven to extinction by the end of the nineteenth century. It somewhat ironically remains a fixture on the state flag, first flown over the nearby Sonoma barracks during the Bear Flag Revolt of 1846.

Mammals commonly found here today include black-tailed deer, raccoons, striped skunks, squirrels, chipmunks, rabbits, field mice, and a host of

Great blue heron. (Photo by Mary Follis.)

other rodents. More reclusive are the bobcat, gray fox, badger, and the rare black bear and mountain lion. Raccoons, skunks, foxes, and deer can be persistent pests in certain coastal campgrounds, so store food in secure containers when not in use.

Birds. For at least part of the year the Sonoma Coast is home to hundreds of species of birds. The more common residents include gulls, cormorants, herons, egrets, pelicans, ospreys, doves, quail, ravens, vultures, hawks, and a wide variety of waterfowl and songbirds. Populations are highest during the fall and spring migrations. Bodega Bay, an important stop along the migration path, is a favorite spot for birdwatching.

Marine Mammals. The most visible marine mammals are the numerous harbor seals that reside along the coast, especially at the mouth of the Russian River. Although they may appear docile, seals frighten easily and can inflict serious bites. They are protected by the Marine Mammal Protection Act, which makes it unlawful to feed, harass, or approach them too closely. Whales, dolphins, porpoises, and sea lions are also protected by this act. On summer weekends, volunteers from the Stewards of Slavianka are normally on hand at Goat Rock Beach to answer questions, loan binoculars, and keep the unwary visitor from approaching the seals too closely.

Bodega Head is an ideal spot to watch the semi-annual migration of the Pacific gray whale. The southward journey occurs in December and January. At the front of the pack are the pregnant females, racing to reach the warm waters of Baja California in time for the birth of their young. They are followed by mature males, nonpregnant females, and finally the juveniles. Calves are born

Harbor seal.

Ocean Safety

The rugged Sonoma coast is known for its beauty, but it can also be dangerous. From 1951 through 1990 there were 88 deaths on the coast, most attributed to drowning. The three most common causes are playing in the surf, fishing, and beachcombing. Scrambling along unstable cliffs and abalone diving in rough weather have also contributed their share of deaths.

A phenomenon called "shore break" is particularly treacherous at beaches such as Goat Rock and Wright's Beach. A deep trench just offshore causes a very shallow wave break. The backwash also goes only as far as the wave break. So a person swept into the sea is pulled out only a short distance before being rushed toward shore, then pulled again back to sea. This "washing machine" effect keeps the victim just out of reach of rescuers on shore. As he is swept parallel to shore, he is eventually dashed onto nearby rocks.

Another danger, especially in fall and winter, are "sleeper waves" generated by storms far out to sea. Multiple sets of waves can overlap as they rush to shore. When the peak of one wave coincides with the trough of another, the sea may look calm and visitors may be lulled into a false sense of security. Then, a set of waves that are "in phase" may roll in, building to a single wave far larger than most. The rush of water from this enormous wave can quickly sweep victims into the surf where rip currents (currents that flow straight out to sea) pull them far into the ocean.

To avoid becoming the next statistic, remember these simple rules:

- Pay attention to the ocean. Never turn your back to it.
- Avoid the beach area between the surf and the high water mark. Never venture into the surf.
- Always have an avenue of escape. When scrambling along rocks, be aware of the tide and return to safety well before you are cut off from the shore.
- If you are caught in a rip current, don't try to swim back against it. Instead, swim parallel to shore until you are out of the current, then swim back to shore.
- Remember that not all of the dangers come from the sea. Many people are killed or injured in falls from cliffs. Follow established trails to the water and stay back from cliff edges.

Divers should remember these additional precautions:

- Before leaving for the coast, call the dive phone at Salt Point State Park, 707-847-3222 to get current ocean swell, visibility, wind, and water temperature. The weather is recorded between 8:00 and 9:00 am daily, with major changes recorded as they occur.
- Upon arrival, check with local park staff or businesses to determine a safe diving location.
- Watch the prospective dive area for at least 20 minutes prior to entering the water to identify water conditions, rip currents, and easy access points. Plan for alternate exits if it becomes rough.
- Always take a float (inner tube, dive mat, dive board, or boat) when you dive.
- Never dive alone.
- Let someone know where you will be diving and when you expect to return.
- Diving is strenuous sport. Be in good physical condition and be sure your gear is in good condition.
- Never enter the water if it is too rough. Your life may depend on it.

the first two weeks in January. The northward migration takes place at a more leisurely pace starting as temperatures rise in February. First to leave are the females who became pregnant on the southern journey, followed by the males. Last to leave, during the month of April, are the new mothers and calves. It is believed that the whales do not feed during the entire migration period and can lose a third of their body weight by the time they return to their Arctic feeding grounds.

Fish and Shellfish. A wide variety of sea life abounds along the coast. In rocky areas, common fish and mollusks include rock cod, ling cod, cabezon, sculpin, abalone, and mussels. Those off sandy beaches include perch, smelt, halibut, sanddabs, and flounder. Clams found in the mud flats of Bodega Harbor include horsenecks, cockles, littlenecks, and Washington. Rock crab and Dungeness crab can also be caught in the Bodega Harbor and jetty area.

Anyone 16 years of age or older who takes any kind of fish, mollusk, amphibian, or crustacean must posess a valid California fishing license. Refer to Fish and Game Regulations for specific information regarding minimum size and limits on specific species. Also, some shellfish, especially mussels, may be poisonous when feeding on the toxic algae that create "red tides" at certain times of the year. Always inquire about quarantines before collecting any shellfish.

Northern California waters are also home to a variety of sharks. The waters around Bodega Bay are at the edge of an important breeding ground for great whites. Seals are a favorite food, and several local attacks have occurred by great whites mistaking a surfer or scuba diver for a seal.

Intertidal Life. The rocky Sonoma shores are host to an abundance of tidal life. Different sets of organisms live in each of the three major intertidal zones. Those with least tolerance to atmospheric exposure live in the low tide zone. More tolerant species live in the mid tide zone, where they may be exposed to air for several hours per day. The most tolerant species live in the high tide zone where they are protected from heavy wave action. Plants and animals of the low tide zone include abalones, sponges, ribbed kelp, anemones, urchins, thatched barnacles, and coralline algae. Those of the mid tide zone include sea palms, mussels, goose barnacles, sea stars, hermit crabs, sea sacks, and aggregated anemones. Periwinkles, limpets, sea lettuce, acorn barnacles, lined shore crabs, and turban snails are typical of life in the high tide zone.

The greatest danger to the intertidal ecology is not the harsh natural environment, but rather the actions of man. Plants and animals exposed to air by the simple act of turning over a rock or moving it higher up the shore will quickly die. Remember these guidelines when exploring tidepool life:

- When looking under rocks, return them to their exact original positions. Animals such as sponges and anemones attached to the underside of rocks will die if left exposed to sun, air, and predators.

- Use a pail or jar to observe free-swimming life, but return it to where you found it when finished.

- Don't try to permanently remove the animals you find. They will quickly die. Remember also that within state parks it is illegal to collect tidepool life.

- The best times for exploring are during low tides. The lowest tides, called spring tides, occur every two weeks near the times of the full moon and new moon. Consult a newspaper for the times of low tides on a particular day. Tide tables for the entire year can be purchased at numerous shops along the coast.

- Dress appropriately. Northern California waters are cold, and the algae-covered rocks are extremely slippery. If you intend to venture any distance from shore, wear waterproof rubber-soled boots or shoes. Pick your way carefully among the rocks and be sure of your footing before taking a step. Consider using a walking staff to help maintain your balance.

- Observe the rules of ocean safety. Stay aware of your surroundings and never turn your back to the sea. Don't let young children explore on their own. Keep track of the incoming tide and return to shore well before your route is cut off by the sea.

For Further Reading

Wilson, Simone, *Sonoma County, the River of Time*, Windsor Publications, Inc., Chatsworth, CA, 1990.

Le Baron, Gaye, and Dee Blackman, Joann Mitchell, and Harvey Hansen, *Santa Rosa, a Nineteenth Century Town*, Historia, Ltd., Santa Rosa, CA, 1985.

Hansen, Harvey, and Jeanne Thurlow Miller, *WIld Oats in Eden, Sonoma County in the 19th Century*, Santa Rosa, 1962.

Wallace, Robert E., editor, *The San Andreas Fault System, California*, United States Geological Survey Professional Paper 1515, U. S. Government Printing Office, Washington, 1990.

Russo, Ron, and Pam Olhausen, *Pacific Intertidal Life, a Guide to Organisms of Rock Reefs and Tide Pools of the Pacific Coast*, Nature Study Guild, Rochester, NY, 1981.

Edwards, Don, *Making the Most of Sonoma County*, Valley of the Moon Press, Alameda, CA, 1986.

Stindt, Fred A., *Trains to the Russian River*, 1974.

Goat Rock and Blind Beach from Blind Beach Trail.

2

Sonoma Coast State Beach

When you first see the empty shores of Sonoma Coast State Beach, you may not believe it is California's fourth most popular state park. In 1996, it hosted over 2.6 million visitors, making it busier than such familiar sites as Point Reyes National Seashore and Mount Tamalpais State Park. Even California's crown jewel, Yosemite National Park, with 4 million visitors, didn't draw many more people. But despite the numbers, don't expect the same crowds here that you'll find at Yosemite. Sonoma Coast's visitors tend to come for only hours rather than days, and when they arrive, they can spread out across 17 miles of cliffs, coves, and beaches. And while the great majority of Yosemite's visitors arrive at the height of summer, Sonoma Coast's are likely to come any time of year.

There is much to do at the park. Enjoy a picnic on an isolated beach, amidst the roar of the breakers and the screeching of gulls. Study tidepools teeming with life in the shadow of an imposing sea stack. Watch gray whales frolic in the sea as they migrate to the warm waters of Baja. Hike the headlands in spring, when wildflowers are a riot of color.

Fast Facts

Internet home page: http://www.mcn.org/1/rrparks/parks/scsb.htm
Park headquarters: Salmon Creek Beach
Hours: Open 24 hrs/day except South Salmon Creek Beach, Bodega Dunes, Wright's Beach, and Russian Gulch, which are day-use only. Camping permitted only at developed campgrounds.
Phone: 707-875-3483
Camping:
Bodega Dunes: open all year, reservations recommended.
Wright's Beach: open all year, reservations recommended.
Willow Creek Environmental Camp: open Apr-Nov, first-come-first-serve.
Pomo Canyon Environmental Camp: open Apr-Nov, first-come-first-serve.
Best hiking trails: Kortum Trail, Dr. David Joseph Memorial Pomo Canyon Trail, Bodega Head Loop, Overlook Trail, Bay Flat Trail, Miwok Loop.

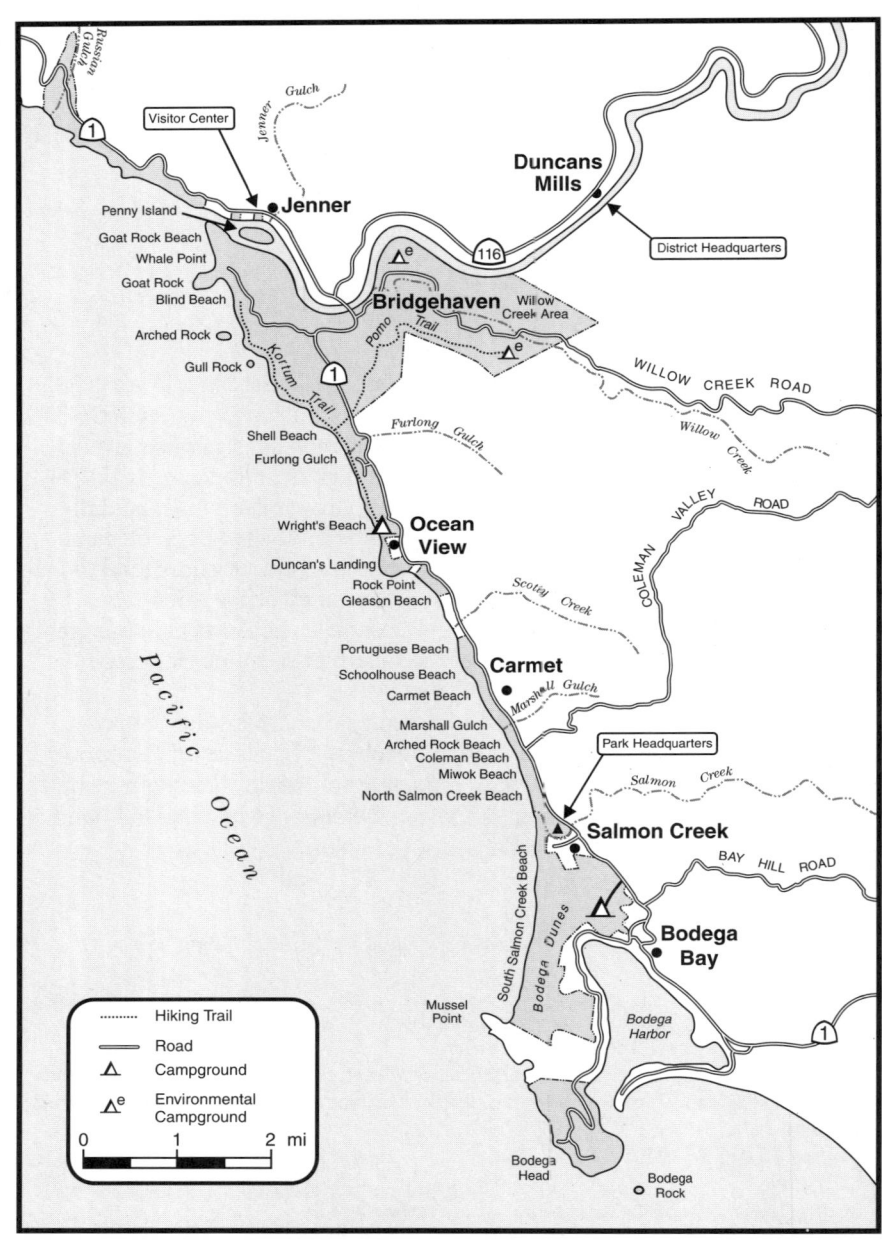

Sonoma Coast State Beach.

One thing you *won't* want to do, though, is swim in the ocean. The frigid waters and strong rip currents make for a dangerous surf. This is also a breeding area for great white sharks, and they have been known to occasionally attack surfers and divers.

Not all of the park is centered around the sea. The secluded Willow Creek area in Pomo Canyon, three miles inland, is a lush grassland surrounded by dense forest. Here you can observe wildlife, hike an old Indian trading path to the coast, or simply find relaxing solitude.

There are two developed campgrounds within the park—at Bodega Dunes and at Wright's Beach. In addition, Willow Creek and Pomo Canyon Environmental Campgrounds offer hike-in campsites for a primitive, "getaway-from-it-all" experience. Bodega Head and most beaches are open 24 hours a day, although camping is permitted only within the campgrounds. South Salmon Creek Beach, Bodega Dunes, Wright's Beach, and Russian Gulch are day-use areas only.

First acquired by the state in 1934, Sonoma Coast's boundaries have been expanded several times. A few stretches of private land still lie interspersed among state properties, so watch for signs and don't trespass, especially near Portuguese Beach, Gleason Beach, and Duncan's Landing.

Historically, Sonoma Coast has been at the forefront of the environmental battleground. For much of the 1960's, a dedicated band waged a protracted but eventually successful battle to stop a nuclear power plant from being built at Bodega Head. In 1972 another battle was waged and won to prevent subdivisions from being built just north of Wright's Beach. Evidence of this fight remains today in the form of a few deserted roads and two houses now owned by the state.

Getting There

There are two main routes to the park. To reach the southern portion, take Bodega Highway west from Sebastopol to its intersection with State Highway 1. Go north four miles to the town of Bodega Bay. All beaches except Bodega Head are accessed directly from the highway north of town. To reach Bodega Head, turn left at East Shore Road on the north side of town.

Another route to the park's northern region is via State Highway 116 west out of Guerneville. When you reach State Highway 1 just south of Jenner, you have two choices. Turn right to reach the Jenner Visitor's Center and coastal access points in Jenner and at Russian Gulch. Turn left and cross the Russian River at Bridgehaven for the beaches at Goat Rock, Shell Beach, and all points south. This is also the way to Willow Creek—from Highway 1, turn left on Willow Creek Road immediately after crossing the Russian River highway bridge.

If you're up for a little adventure, Coleman Valley Road offers breathtaking views of the coast. This narrow, winding road out of Occidental was

Supplemental Park Rules

The following information supplements the general rules for California State Parks listed on Page 12.

Day Use Fees. At present, the day use areas are not subject to fees except at Bodega Dunes, Wright's Beach, Willow Creek, and Pomo Canyon. At times in the past, the state has attempted to start collecting fees at all beaches, but the inevitable public outcry has always caused them to reconsider.

Camping. Camping is allowed only in designated campsites. There are developed campgrounds at Bodega Dunes and Wright's Beach and walk-in environmental campgrounds at Willow Creek and Pomo Canyon. All are subject to fees. The developed campgrounds are open all year, and sites may be reserved by calling toll-free at 800-444-7275. Although reservations are not required, they are strongly advised, especially in the summer. The environmental camps, open April through November, aren't on the reservation system but are first-come-first-serve.

Animals. All animals within the park are protected from molestation and injury. State Fish and Game regulations govern all activities above mean high tide. Within this authority, tidepool creatures are also protected. Separate Federal laws protect marine mammals (see Page 14.)

Collecting. All living and non-living things are protected within the park and may not be collected. You must obtain a permit from the district superintendent for any exceptions. Geological and archaeological features are also protected. The somewhat arcane rules on driftwood allow you to collect up to 50 pounds plus one piece. You can't use chain saws and must hand carry it out.

Pets. Animals must be kept leashed and under control at all times. Certain areas are closed to dogs, including the mouth of the Russian River both north and south, the environmental camps, and the bluffs on Bodega Head. Dogs are not allowed on trails.

Fires. At present, controlled fires smaller than 3'x3' are allowed on the beaches. (This may change in the future.) Fires in the dunes and dune grasses are prohibited, as well as fires in an area with any type of vegetation.

Horses. Horses are not allowed on beaches except for the beach south of the Bodega Dunes day use area. A horse staging area is located off Bay Flat Road.

Off-Highway Vehicles. No vehicles, including mountain bikes, are allowed off road in the park.

Curfew. Juveniles under 18 years of age are not allowed on the beaches after sunset unless accompanied by their parent or guardian.

once voted the most scenic drive in Sonoma County. It is little more than one lane wide for much of its length, making it unsuitable for recreational vehicles or vehicles with trailers. The road reaches Highway 1 just north of Coleman Beach. Save this drive for a clear day when you can clearly see the spectacular coastline. A tip: you'll better appreciate the views by driving toward the ocean rather than away from it.

Natural Environment

You can think of Sonoma Coast State Beach as four distinct regions: Bodega Head, Bodega Dunes, the northern coast, and the Willow Creek area. Each has a distinct natural environment. Bodega Head is an exposed, brush-covered, rocky headland, while Bodega Dunes has some of the most expansive sand dunes in the state. The coast north of Bodega Bay alternates between sandy beaches and rocky bluffs, while the Willow Creek area consists of grasslands surrounded by dense forest.

Bodega Head

The erosion-resistant granite of Bodega Head stands in stark contrast to the marine sediments lying east of the harbor. Separated by the San Andreas Fault, its rocks are geologically unrelated to those inland. Over the last 30 million years the Head has moved hundreds of miles northward. It now stands as the last exposure of granitic basement rock along the coast north of San Francisco. Other exposures include Point Reyes and the Farallon Islands.

One weekend each April, Bodega Bay celebrates the annual Fishermans Festival. Two days of celebration include barbeques, live music, bathtub races, and a fine arts show and crafts fair. Events culminate in a parade of colorfully decorated fishing boats and the blessing of the fleet by local clergymen. Bodega Head is a popular spot to watch the festivities. Crowds can be enormous, so get there early for a good spot. For more information, call the Bodega Bay Area Visitor's Center at 707-875-3422.

Directions

Take Highway 1 to the north side of Bodega Bay. Turn west at the large sign labeled "Bodega Head–Westside Park–Marinas" at East Shore Road. Follow the road down the hill and turn right at the stop sign. This is Bay Flat Road, which becomes West Shore Road at a large dirt parking area on the right. (If you have horses, you can park here and ride the trail to Bodega Dunes.) Campbell Cove sits at the southern end of the road, three miles from the stop sign. To reach the rocky headlands, continue around the hairpin turn sharply right and up the hill. Bodega Head is open 24 hours but no overnight camping is allowed.

Campbell Cove

It's hard to imagine any sane person wanting to build a nuclear power plant atop the San Andreas Fault, but that's exactly what the Pacific Gas and Electric Company once tried to do at Campbell Cove. Without any public hearings they began construction in 1958. The outraged citizens of Bodega Bay, led by the feisty Rose Gaffney, immediately rallied to stop the work.

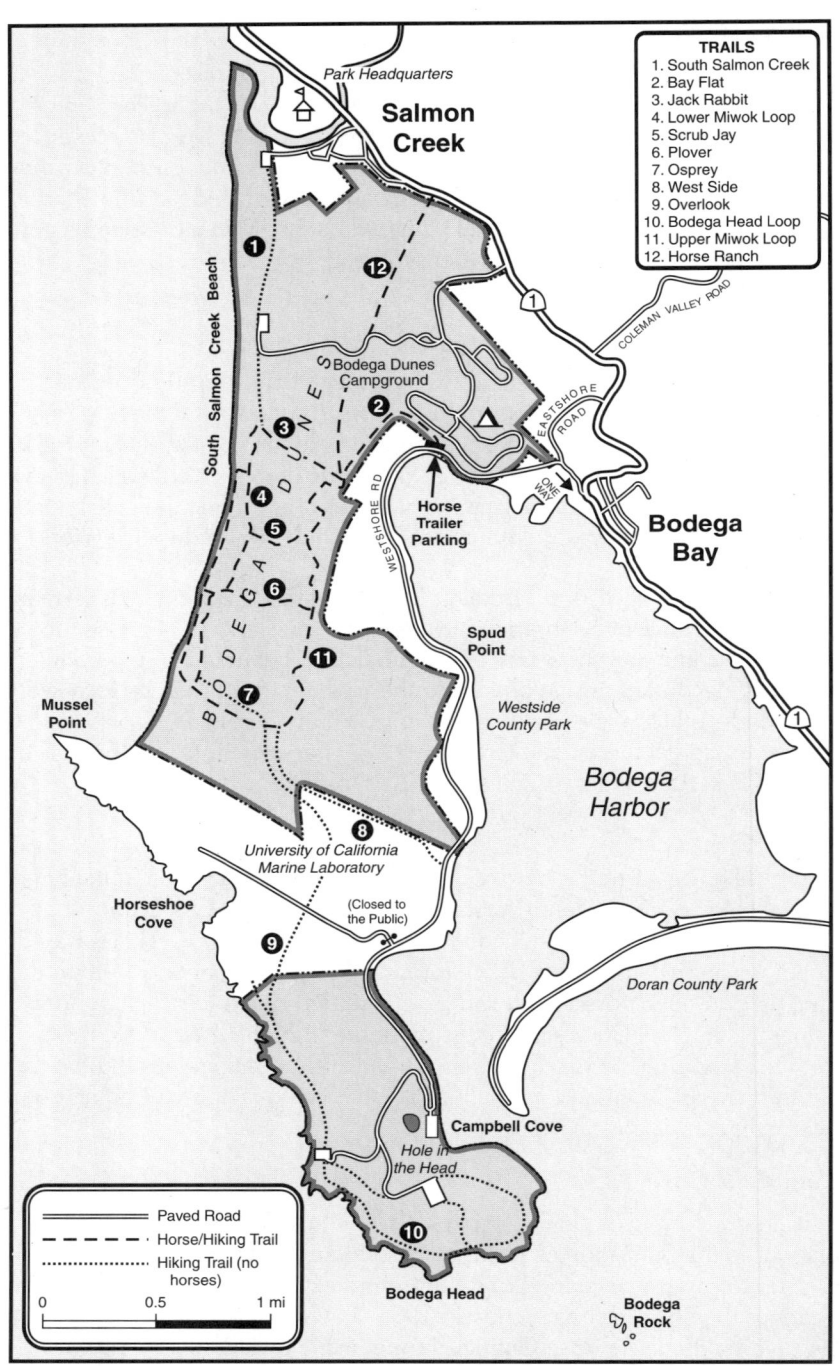

Bodega Harbor area.

Campbell Cove, where Francis Drake may have landed in 1579, is a favorite spot for families with small children.

The ensuing legal battles lasted a decade, but sanity eventually prevailed. Today, the only remaining evidence of this aborted project is a water-filled excavation pit known as Hole-in-the-Head.

Campbell Cove has recently emerged as a credible contender for the site of Sir Francis Drake's landfall in 1579. Author Brian Kelleher, in his well-researched book, *Drake's Bay*, has cited a number of convincing arguments, including the quality of its harbor, its match to Drake's recorded latitude, and the fact that the surrounding land is similar to his description of the landing site. Unfortunately, excavation work for the nuclear power plant probably destroyed any remaining archeological evidence, so scholars will undoubtedly continue to argue these points for decades to come.

Campbell Cove has a large dirt parking lot, picnic tables, and a wooden outhouse. Its sheltered, sandy beach is perfect for families. At low tide, the mudflats here are an excellent spot for catching crabs or digging clams.

Headlands Area

After Campbell Cove, the road winds 0.4 mile to a Y intersection. The right fork leads to the west parking lot overlooking the Pacific. The left fork leads to the east parking lot overlooking the harbor. Cinderblock outhouses are located at both parking lots, but there are no picnic tables here.

In winter and early spring, the west lot is a favorite spot for gray whale watching. The southern migration in December and January tends to occur some distance off shore, so the best sightings usually occur during the more leisurely northern migration from February through April. On weekends during the season, volunteers from the Stewards of Slavianka are available to help watch for spouts, answer questions about the migration, and discuss the natural history of the whale.

Bodega Head Hiking Trails

Two main hiking trails branch out from the parking lots at the Head. The Bodega Head Loop winds around the rocky headlands while the Overlook

From December through April, Bodega Head is a good spot to watch for gray whales as they migrate along the coast. On many weekend afternoons, volunteers from the Stewards of Slavianka are available to help visitors learn more about the whales as they watch for telltale spouts.

Trail stretches from the Head to South Salmon Creek Beach. Both offer breathtaking views of the coast and, in spring and summer, a profusion of colorful wildflowers. For much of their lengths they are exposed as they traverse the headlands, so save these hikes for a clear day when winds aren't too strong. Neither trail is open to horses or mountain bikes.

Bodega Head Loop. This trail departs from the southwest corner of the west parking lot near the outhouses. The 1.5-mile loop spans the southern tip of the Head. It hugs the cliff edges for most of its distance, so keep young children in control. From December through April, you may be lucky enough to glimpse the spouts of California gray whales as they migrate along the coast. At several points along the way, you'll see sheltered beaches 150 feet below you, but the faint volunteer trails down to them aren't maintained by the state and descent is dangerous. Stay on the loop trail—if you really want to frolic in the sand, head for one of the northern beaches.

After about a half mile of easy hiking, a spur trail branches left to the 204-foot summit. On a clear day, this vantage point offers spectacular 360-degree views of the Sonoma and Marin coasts. Bodega Rock rises from the sea in the southern foreground, while the Point Reyes peninsula stretches across the horizon behind it. From here you can return the way you came to the main loop or proceed along the spur trail for the shortest path to the east parking lot. If you continue around the main loop, you'll cross wildflower-covered headlands before reaching an immense cow parsnip forest that ends near the east parking lot. In the spring and summer, the white-flowered shoots of these members of the carrot family can climb as high as 10 feet into the air.

At the east lot you'll find excellent views of the harbor and Campbell Cove. You also look down on the fenced-off remains of the infamous Hole-in-the-Head. From this lot, follow the road 0.2 mile to a driveway on your left with a gate to block vehicles. Go around the gate and take the single-track trail northeast toward your starting point. The path leads to an isolated

Bodega Marine Reserve. Horseshoe Cove is in the foreground.

stand of cypress whose tangled branches form a natural fort for children. It's an easy walk from here back to the west lot.

Overlook Trail. This trail leads 2.5 miles from Bodega Head to Salmon Creek Beach across headlands covered with ice plant, purple seaside daisies, bush lupine, and coastal scrub/grasslands. Pick up the trail at the northeast corner of the west parking lot. As you climb the crest of the bluff, you'll have excellent views of the coast on your left and the harbor on your right. From December through April, keep an eye open for migrating whales.

Part of this trail traverses the Bodega Marine Reserve, a 326-acre laboratory operated by the University of California. The Reserve is otherwise off-limits to the public, so obey the posted signs and stay on the trail along this portion. You can visit the lab when it is open to the public on Fridays from 2 to 4 pm—take the marked road west off West Shore Road.

About 0.3 mile from the trailhead, you come to a short spur trail on your left. This path gives you a good view of Horseshoe Cove and the lab on Marine Reserve property, but the marine lab staff ask that you not proceed past the overlook.

Returning to the main trail, you begin a steady descent, eventually reaching Marine Reserve property. You should stay on the trail while you traverse this property. As you hike this stretch, notice the terrain change from coastal scrub to grass-covered dunes. Follow the trail markers to reach the southern end of the beach. From here, you can either return the way you came or continue along the Bodega Dunes trails for a longer hike.

Bodega Dunes

Just north of Bodega Head are the sands of Bodega Dunes. These expansive dunes stretch from Bodega Harbor to Salmon Creek, rising as high as 200 feet above the sea. With luck, you may see several of the many species of mammals that reside here, including jackrabbits, voles, mice, badgers, raccoons, and foxes.

The dunes were heavily overgrazed by cattle in the late 1800's, almost completely stripping them of vegetation. Without the stabilizing influence of native plants, the sand began shifting and eventually threatened Bodega Harbor. In 1951 a dune stabilization project was started. Various specialized grasses were planted to help keep drifting sands from silting up the harbor. Even today the restoration is not complete, so stay off the sand in fenced-off areas.

Both a campground and a day-use area are located at Bodega Dunes. A wheelchair-accessible boardwalk crosses the dunes from the day-use parking lot to the beach. Please stay on designated paths as you explore this area. Because of the extreme danger, no fires are permitted in the dunes.

Directions

The easiest way to the dunes is via the Bodega Dunes Campground road. From Highway 1, turn west at the sign marking the campground. Pay your entrance fee at the kiosk 0.4 mile west of the highway. You can then turn right and go 0.8 mile to the day use parking area or proceed ahead to the campground.

You can also reach the northernmost dunes from the hamlet of Salmon Creek. Follow the directions on Page 31 for South Salmon Creek Beach and walk the boardwalk across the dunes. Stay on the path and avoid the fenced-off dune restoration areas.

Bodega Dunes Campground

The campground is situated well back from the beach, sheltered by the dunes and stands of eucalyptus and cypress. Three loop roads contain a total of 98 campsites. The upper campground, sites 1-21, backs up to a eucalyptus grove that is home to thousands of Monarch butterflies for a short period each fall. Facilities include restrooms with flush toilets, running water, hot showers (the only ones in the park), picnic tables, and a trailer sanitation dump. Reservations are accepted all year through the state park reservation service at 1-800-444-7275, and are strongly advised in the summer.

Day-Use Area

From the day-use parking lot it is only a short hike along the boardwalk over low dunes to South Salmon Creek Beach. Various trails extend along the shore and up into the grass- and ice plant-covered dunes. If you hike all the way to Mussel Point at the south end of the beach, remember that the point itself is part of the private Bodega Marine Reserve and is closed to public access.

Riders pick their way through the soft sands of Bodega Dunes.

Equestrian Access

The northern part of the beach is reserved for foot traffic, so if you have horses, you need to approach the dunes from the west side off Bay Flat Road. There is a free parking area for horse trailers 0.3 mile west of the junction with East Shore Road. Horses are permitted on Salmon Creek Beach only up to the boardwalk. No dogs are allowed on the trail.

Bodega Dunes Trails

A number of trails wind throughout the dunes, which are broader and higher than they might first seem. It is easy to get lost, and while you are unlikely to be in any real danger, you may find yourself taking a much longer hike than you anticipated. Shortly before this book went to press, I stopped at the Salmon Creek Ranger Station and happened to mention how easily someone could get lost on these trails. The rangers concurred and pointed to a stack of brand new trail signs patiently awaiting the resources necessary to post them. Perhaps by the time you read this they will be up and ready to guide you along your way.

The following trails are only a sampling of those you will want to explore.

Bay Flat Trail. Hikers may be tempted to avoid this trail because it is a main horse path to the dunes, but don't be discouraged. On a sunny Saturday in June, I didn't encounter another person, either on horseback or on foot, during my entire hike. The trail begins at the equestrian parking lot on Bay Flat Road, so if there aren't a lot of horse trailers parked there, you should be safe enough.

The route starts at the north end of the lot, just past a portable outhouse. The level ground quickly turns to deep sand visibly churned by horses' hooves. On your right is the campground, while on your left is private property. The path then turns southwest and quickly climbs 100 feet up the back of the dunes. You continue through rolling dunes covered with grass and yellow bush lupine until reaching the juncture with Upper Miwok Loop trail.

Miwok Loop Trail. You can enter this loop from any of a number of spots. Besides the junction with Bay Flat Trail, others include South Salmon Creek Trail out of the Bodega Dunes day-use area, West Side Trail from West Shore Road, and Overlook Trail from Bodega Head.

Probably the easiest starting point is the day-use area at Bodega Dunes. Take the paved trail to the wooden boardwalk, then on to the beach. (The boardwalk is wheelchair-accessible up to an observation deck.) At the beach, turn south and hike toward Mussel Point, 1.5 miles away. As you walk along the sand, pay attention to the surf. If it isn't too rough and you're not there at high tide, you can walk the upper edges of the compacted sand, staying well away from the breakers. Otherwise you're safest if you walk in the soft sand above the high water line. (This is slower and more strenuous, so plan your hike accordingly.)

Heading south, you'll notice several trails up into the dunes. (If you're not up for a long hike, you can take any of these to a return trail, Lower Miwok Loop, behind the foredunes.) Continue along the beach about a mile to a sign with the word "trail" pointing up the dune. Follow the sign to quickly connect with Lower Miwok Loop just south of Plover Trail. Turn right and walk along the soft sand. Notice the dense vegetation, including native yellow bush lupine as well as various introduced grasses and ice plant, that help stabilize the shifting dunes. You soon come to a signed three-way intersection. You can continue straight ahead to Westside Park, turn right to Bodega Head and the beach, or turn left to Bodega Dunes Campground. The described route turns left, heading east and eventually north.

After another mile or so hiking generally northward, you reach the junction with Jack Rabbit Trail. Head west just over a quarter of a mile to another junction. Take the right fork to reach the campground road and continue another 0.1 mile to the parking lot. The total length of the full hike approaches 4 miles.

Northern Coast

The most popular part of the park runs from Salmon Creek north past the mouth of the Russian River. Highway 1 runs right along the edge of the bluffs here, giving you easy beach access at numerous points. The more popular beaches tend to have large parking lots and reasonably easy trails. Some spots have narrow trails that cling precariously to the cliff sides, while a few have only the faintest hint of a trail. Use common sense and don't try to descend unless you're sure it is safe. Remember that the coast is unforgiving, and a moment of carelessness could have tragic consequences.

For most of this distance, the park extends from Highway 1 to the sea, but there are still several stretches of private property interspersed along the way. These include the land between Portuguese Beach and Gleason Beach, at Rock Point, at Ocean View, and the houses on the bluff above Goat Rock. Don't trespass in these areas.

South Salmon Creek Beach

This broad, sandy beach, flanked by Bodega Dunes, extends over 2 miles from Salmon Creek to Mussel Point. The most northerly access is by way of Bean Avenue in the hamlet of Salmon Creek. The parking lot at the end of the road is usually full on nice days, especially on weekend afternoons.

You won't see any indication of beach access from the highway, so watch for the turn-off just south of the Salmon Creek bridge. The narrow road meanders through a residential area reminiscent of a New England fishing village. Keep to the right, staying on Bean Avenue, and drive all the way to the free parking lot at the end of the road. From 7 pm Friday to 6 am Monday, parking is not allowed on the road until you reach this parking lot on state park property. From here, hike over a broad expanse of grass-covered dunes to the beach.

North Salmon Creek Beach

This is one of the most popular spots along the entire Sonoma Coast. It has plenty of free parking, easy coastal access, and a long sandy beach that's great for picnicking, kite-flying, frisbee-throwing, and surf fishing. On hot summer weekends parking is at a premium, and this beach can resemble the crowded ones of Southern California. Even in winter you'll rarely be alone—I counted over two dozen people here on a cold December afternoon with storm seas raging and angry clouds threatening a deluge at any

Equestrians ride along South Salmon Creek Beach. Horses must stay south of the boardwalk.

A couple takes in the view from a lonely point along the Kortum Trail.

moment. At any time of year you are likely to see wet-suit clad surfers riding the waves here.

Several parking areas dot this stretch of the highway. Some are paved, some just gravel pull-outs at the side of the road. The best is a large paved lot just north of milepost 12.75. It has two cinderblock restrooms on its east side with motorhome-style flush toilets, but no running water. A paved trail from the restrooms leads down to the Salmon Creek estuary. When the creek mouth silts up, it forms a broad lagoon that is a favorite roost for a variety of shorebirds. Some of the species you may see include gulls, herons, egrets, sandpipers, loons, and pelicans. There is an easy trail at the west end of this lot leading directly to the beach 30 feet below.

Miwok Beach

This pleasant sandy beach is named after the Miwok Indians that originally inhabited the southern Sonoma Coast. Its small parking area is well-marked and directly adjacent to the highway. You won't find any restrooms here. A steep but relatively easy asphalt trail leads 60 feet down to the beach. At one point the asphalt is paved directly atop a corrugated metal culvert over a seasonal creek. Luckily, it is more sturdy than it first appears. Stone steps at the bottom of the trail simplify access to the beach.

The southern edge of Miwok Beach merges with North Salmon Creek Beach. At low tide you can easily walk the full distance to Salmon Creek, but the beach shrinks considerably at high tide.

Coleman Beach

For some reason the parking area at this beach is not marked. Watch for a small paved lot just south of highway milepost 13.46. A narrow asphalt trail winds precariously down the side of an 80-foot cliff covered with ice plant, purple seaside daisies, and cow parsnip. It ends in a wooden staircase, and to reach the sandy beach you have to scramble over the rocky talus at the

Limpets cling to a boulder at Arched Rock Beach.

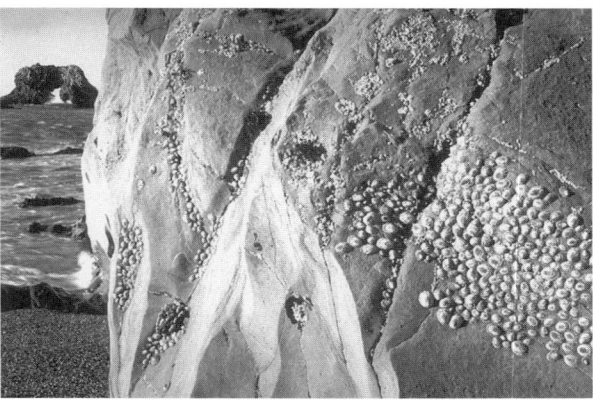

base of the cliff. At high tide the beach can be submerged while the surf comes right up to the staircase. When the tide recedes you may be able to walk all the way south to Salmon Creek. Look for a scenic waterfall cascading down the cliff north of this beach after seasonal rains.

Arched Rock Beach

A large parking lot on a bluff directly off the highway provides excellent views of the rocky coast to the north and Salmon Creek Beach to the south. A very poor trail, not maintained by the state, leads part way down the cliff, but heavy rains in February 1998, the wettest month in Sonoma County history, nearly obliterated the bottom half. If you really want to ignore common sense and scramble down to this beach, wear hiking boots or good athletic shoes, use your hands and knees to pick your way down the loose cliffs, and don't blame me if you fall and break your neck. Once down, you'll find a small isolated beach consisting of polished, multicolored pea gravel. The namesake rock, an offshore sea stack with a hole in the middle, is visible a few hundred feet to the north. (Note that this is not the same Arched Rock that is prominent further north near Blind Beach.) This beach is nearly gone at high tide, so keep track of the tide before climbing down. There are no restrooms at this beach.

Marshall Gulch

You'll find a sheltered, sandy beach (obscured at high tide) on the south side of the gulch. The rocky north side nominally connects to Carmet Beach, but hiking over the slippery rocks is difficult and dangerous even at low tide. There is a small, paved parking area on a bluff just north of the gulch. Arched Rock lies directly west, but because of its angle, you can't see the arch from here. A good but narrow paved trail leads down to the beach.

Carmet Beach

Two trails from this parking area lead 80 feet down to beaches. A good trail on the south side leads right down to a small sandy beach. Another trail on the north side leads to a somewhat larger sandy beach having a rocky surfline. You'll see much evidence of crumbling cliffs at the base of this beach. These are good spots for tidepooling.

Schoolhouse Beach

A large parking lot here can hold dozens of cars in a sort of free-for-all arrangement. The deep, isolated beach is on the north side of the lot. An easy trail connects with a gravel access road (closed to vehicles) about half way down. A dual cinderblock outhouse sits at this juncture. This is another favorite spot for tidepooling.

Portuguese Beach

This popular beach is about half a mile long and deep enough that it is still accessible even at high tide. The large parking area is on a bluff at the south side of the beach. Two trails lead down to the beach. The one closest to the highway is a very easy, wide gravel road that ends high up on the sand. A cinderblock outhouse is located here. The more westerly trail is much steeper, with switchbacks and many steps, but ends right at the surf. In fact, the last several wooden steps are held by wire cables designed to let them float at high tide.

Gleason Beach

A sign proclaiming Gleason Beach marks this small parking lot on a bluff 100 feet above the ocean, but don't expect to reach the beach here. There are a few scattered remnants of an old trail at the south end of the lot, including an overgrown sign part way down the cliff warning of the dangers of sleeper waves, but the lower half of the trail was destroyed by a storm and is not scheduled to be repaired. If you look carefully, you can still see faint

Anglers try their luck at Duncan's Cove.

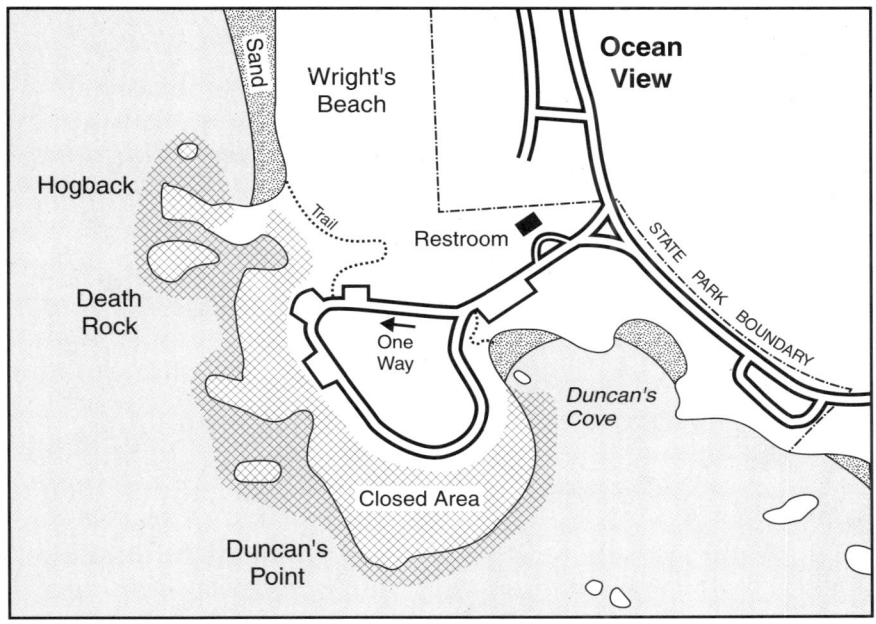

Wright's Beach

Ocean View

Hogback

Trail

Restroom

Death Rock

One Way

STATE PARK BOUNDARY

Duncan's Cove

Closed Area

Duncan's Point

Duncan's Landing. Stay away from the posted danger area.

traces of the old asphalt path down the side of the cliff. They abruptly end less than half way down, so don't try to climb down to the beach. Instead, stay in the parking lot, enjoy the views, and admire the large sea stack directly across from you.

Rock Point

This is a good spot for a short rest to relax and view the rugged coastline. Two small dirt parking lots just off the highway provide excellent views of the rocky shoreline. Each lot has a single picnic table. There are no restrooms and no beach access from here.

Duncan's Landing

This rocky promontory shelters a cove that was once a doghole port for lumber schooners. Wright's Beach is to the north and Duncan's Cove to the south. From 1862 to 1877, Samuel and Alexander Duncan used a horse-drawn railway to deliver lumber to the landing from their mill at Bridge-haven on the Russian River. Schooners were loaded using a wooden slide chute that extended down from the cliff.

Eventually, the narrow-gauge railroad pushed through from Occidental to the Russian River, so the Duncan brothers moved to the present site of Duncans Mills and shipped their lumber by rail. After that, the port was still used to ship such staples as butter, potatoes, and vegetables. During Prohibition, it was a favorite anchorage for rumrunners.

A short, paved access road leads from the highway to the rocky point. There it becomes a one-way loop with several parking areas. A good trail at the north end of the loop leads 80 feet down to Wright's Beach. Directly off the point are two large sea stacks—an onshore stack called the Hogback and an island known as Death Rock. It didn't come by that name accidentally, for Death Rock is one of the most deadly spots along the entire California coast. Even though the entire shoreline around Duncan's Landing, including Death Rock, is closed to public access, it still manages to claim at least one victim nearly every year.

Along the access road is another parking area and trail down the south side of the point to Duncan's Cove. This trail was improved in 1996 and now includes a wooden staircase right down to the beach. Restrooms, partially hidden by trees, are located across the road from this trailhead.

Wright's Beach

This popular beach consists of a picnic area and campground at the end of a short paved road winding down to the beach. Restrooms in the campground provide running water and flush toilets but no showers. Both the beach and the restrooms are wheelchair-accessible.

This is one of the few spots in the park where day-use fees are collected. The parking area and picnic tables lie directly back from the beach, buffered by a low ridge of dune grass. The wide, sandy beach stretches for over a mile and is popular with fishermen, divers, and beachcombers. Obey posted signs and stay away from Death Rock at the south end of the beach.

The 30-site campground lies north of the parking lot, partially protected by trees and shrubs. Campsites are closely spaced but separated by bushes to give some sense of privacy. The more northerly sites back directly up to the beach. It is a pleasant enough campground on a calm day, but when the wind picks up you'll be happier in the confines of an RV rather than being buffeted in a tent. The campground, designated as "premium" by the park system, is on the reservation system all year. Reservations are strongly advised during the summer. Call the state park reservation service at 1-800-444-7275, to reserve a campsite.

Wright's Beach is the southern terminus of the Kortum Trail, a four-mile long seaside path along the headlands that starts near Goat Rock.

Furlong Gulch

You won't see a parking area anywhere near Furlong Gulch, nor even a road sign to mark its presence, but if you know how to get there, you'll find an excellent isolated beach surrounded by high bluffs. When I was there one sunny winter afternoon there wasn't another soul in site, not even footprints

Hikers march single file along the Kortum Trail at Furlong Gulch.

on the coarse dark sand. It's the perfect spot for getting away from it all. (But don't expect isolation on a summer weekend!)

The Kortum Trail crosses here barely 50 feet from the beach, so you can park at Shell Beach and make an easy half-mile hike south to the gulch. The wildflowers along this trail can be spectacular in the spring. But beware— during the rainy season the gulch can be an impassible torrent of water.

An even easier access is from the south. Drive to milepost 17.65 and turn west on Carlevaro Way, part of an abandoned subdivision now owned by the state. The two houses to the south are homes for state park staff. Don't disturb the residents; instead, turn right onto Grill Way and park at the end of the road. From here, a path leads west a short distance to connect with the Kortum Trail. Hike north a few hundred feet until the trail descends the side of the gully, then head west to the beach.

Shell Beach

If your interest leans toward beachcombing and tidepool exploration, this is the spot to go. The rocky north end nurtures a host of marine life and is frequently used by elementary schools as an outdoor classroom. There is also a sandy beach to the south that is popular for fishing and picnicking.

From the large Shell Beach sign on the highway, follow a short paved road to a large parking lot with a dual cinderblock outhouse at its west end. From here, a 500-foot long trail winds down the bluff to the beach. The trail is reasonably easy as it descends to the beach except at its very end. Children and less athletic adults will probably need a hand to get down the last six feet.

The tidepools are best explored at low tide, so check a local newspaper or consult a tide table before your trip. Once there, use caution when climbing over the slippery, algae-covered rocks. Be sure to obey the rules of ocean safety listed on Page 15 and review the section on intertidal life starting on Page 16. Some of the organisms found here include limpets, mussels, turban snails, anemones, sea stars, chitons, sea urchins, hermit crabs, and shore crabs. Remember that tidepool life is protected within the park, so try to return anything you pick up (including rocks with sea life attached) to the exact position you found it. Fishermen need a valid California sport fishing license in their possession and may only take those species designated in the current California Sport Fishing Regulations.

Blind Beach

Yet another long sandy beach, this one is a good spot for smelt fishing, beachcombing, and solitary strolls. The northern end adjacent to the Goat Rock parking lot is easily accessed and therefore more heavily visited. If you're looking for more solitude and don't mind a hike, you should enter from the Blind Beach parking lot, 0.75 mile down Goat Rock Road. The trail meanders 0.5 mile down to the southern end of the beach 200 feet below (be careful—poison oak grows profusely along the trailside). In spring and summer, many wildflowers bloom along this trail. A pair of dilapidated cinderblock outhouses sit at the north end of the parking lot next to the trailhead.

Goat Rock Beach

This is one of the of the most popular spots in the park. Goat Rock boasts long sandy beaches, two parking lots, and a picnic area with fire rings. At the extreme north end of the beach you'll usually find a colony of harbor seals lounging lazily on the sand. On weekends, volunteers from the Stewards of Slavianka are on hand with binoculars and spotting scopes to help you safely observe them. They can also answer many questions about the seals and their habitat.

Female seals give birth to pups between March and June. A pup sometimes appears to be abandoned, but don't worry. It has generally been left behind only temporarily while the mother forages for food. Keep your distance—not only is it against the law to harass the seals, you'll find that both adults and pups can inflict serious bites. A raised head can be a signal of alarm and distress for a seal, not always mere curiosity.

In the early 20th century, countless tons of rock were hauled over these railroad tracks at Goat Rock Beach to help build a breakwater at the mouth of the Russian River.

Goat Rock itself looks like an enormous sea stack, but until the 1920's it was actually a peninsula. Rock from the bluff was quarried down to the height of the current parking lot to help form a breakwater at the mouth of the Russian River. You can still see, on the north end of Goat Rock Beach, the rusted remains of the railway used to haul away the rock.

To reach Goat Rock Beach, turn west from Highway 1 at the large wooden sign near milepost 19.15. Follow the road to its end, where it branches in two directions. The left fork leads to the north end of Blind Beach and to Goat Rock, named for the herds of goats that lived here while it was still a peninsula. The parking lot here extends from shore all the way to the rock. (For safety reasons, Goat Rock itself is closed to the public.) The right fork leads down to the beach parking lot and picnic area. There are metal fire rings here for picnickers. It is only a short hike over low dunes to the beach, but a good 500 yards north to the seal colony.

Arched Rock View

In the water off Blind Beach is an enormous sea stack with a huge hole in it. Called Arched Rock on maps, it is much larger than the rock to the south for which Arched Rock Beach is named. In fact it is so large that intrepid kayakers have been known to paddle through it when seas are calm—not something to be recommended here, however.

The Arched Rock View parking area, 1.25 miles down Goat Rock Road, gives you an excellent view of this arch.

Jenner

Stop at the Jenner Visitor's Center for the latest information on park activities, seal and whale activity, and general information on the coast. You'll also find a number of books, postcards, and clothing related to the coast. The center, open weekends from 10-4, is located in a historic former boathouse directly across the road from the service station/convenience store. John Easdale, a renowned boat builder, made beautifully-crafted canoes and rowboats here in the 1930's and 40's.

There are several coastal access point just north of town. The most popular trail leads from a small dirt parking area just north of milepost 22.24. Hike 80 feet down the moderately steep trail to a long, sandy beach on the north side of the Russian River. You can get an excellent view of the seal colony—usually across the river, but sometimes on this side. Remember to stay back approximately 50 feet and do not disturb the animals. (If they are raising their heads you are too close.)

For a panoramic view of the coast, stop at one of the two dirt pull-outs near milepost 22.53. If you are reasonably athletic, you may want to walk to a peak formed by a highway cut just north of the parking area. From here, follow a narrow, overgrown trail around the west side of the peak and then

	FACILITIES											ACTIVITIES										
	Fee Area	Camping - Developed	Camping - Environmental	Restrooms	Showers	Trailer Sanitary Station	Telephone	Picnic Area	Visitor's Center	Beach Access	Disabled Access	Hiking	Horseback Riding	Mountain Biking	Tidepooling	Whale Watching	Seal Watching	Ocean Fishing	Freshwater Fishing	Surfing	Scuba Diving/Snorkeling	Sea Kayaking
Bodega Head				●				●		●		●			●	●		●			●	
Campbell Cove				●				●		●		●						●				●
Bodega Dunes	●	●		●	●	●	●	●		●	●	●	●					●				
South Salmon Creek Beach				●				●		●		●						●		●		
North Salmon Creek Beach				●				●		●								●		●		
Miwok Beach										●								●		●		
Coleman Beach										●					●			●				
Arched Rock Beach																		●				
Marshall Gulch										●				Paved	●			●			●	
Carmet Beach										●					●			●			●	
Schoolhouse Beach				●				●		●					●			●		●		
Portuguese Beach				●				●		●					●			●		●		
Gleason Beach														Roads								
Rock Point								●														
Duncan's Landing				●				●		●	●							●				●
Wright's Beach	●	●		●			●	●		●	●	●						●		●		
Furlong Gulch										●		●						●				●
Shell Beach				●						●		●		Only	●			●			●	
Blind Beach				●						●		●						●		●	●	
Goat Rock Beach				●			●	●		●							●	●		●		●
Arched Rock View																						
Jenner				●			●	●	●	●						●			●	●	●	●
Russian Gulch				●				●		●		●						●			●	●
Willow Creek	●		●	●				●		●									●			
Pomo Canyon	●		●	●				●				●										
Vista Trail				●				●		●	●							●				

steeply down. Descend carefully to an exposed granite promontory with spectacular views. Goat Rock Beach and the Russian River mouth lie to the south, while views of the rocky coastline lie to the north. Save this hike for a time when the winds aren't too strong.

Russian Gulch

The parking area for Russian Gulch is just over two miles north of Jenner. Watch for the dirt road on the west side of the highway near milepost 24.55. A gate at the entrance closes at sunset or when the rangers get around to it. The trail leaves from the end of the lot just past the pit toilet. It's a 0.3 mile hike through alders, willows, and dense underbrush to the beach. Although level, this hike definitely isn't for everyone. You'll find yourself wishing for a machete as you scramble over and under twisted tree branches at numerous points along the way. (But leave the machete at home—it's illegal!) When you reach the beach, make a mental note of the trail location, as it may not be obvious when you're ready to leave. The isolated beach is sheltered by tall cliffs on either side. Several picnic tables sit on a sandy bench south of the creek.

Northern Hiking Trails

You'll have impressive views from any of the northern area's three main hiking trails. Kortum Trail and Vista Trail are relatively easy walks, while the Pomo Canyon Trail is more strenuous. Be sure to take along water, snacks, and protection from sun and wind. Horses and mountain bikes are not allowed on any of these trails.

Kortum Trail. In spring and summer, the coastal headlands along this reasonably easy, 4-mile trail from Blind Beach to Wright's Beach are blanketed with a spectactular explosion of wildflowers. Some of the numerous types you'll see include Douglas iris, buttercup, sticky monkey-flower, cow parsnip, flowering currant, purple bush lupine, Indian paintbrush, salmonberry, purple seaside daisy, coast buckwheat, and sea thrift. The trail is named for former Sonoma County Supervisor Bill Kortum. In the early 1970's he helped lead the effort to stop construction of housing developments that would have destroyed the natural beauty of this coast.

The trail's northern end starts at the Blind Beach parking lot, 0.8 mile down the road to Goat Rock. (If you prefer a shorter hike, park at the dirt parking area 0.3 mile down the road.) Head south along the road a few hundred feet to the trailhead. You quickly climb 100 feet as you pass Peaked Hill on your left, then begin a steady 200-foot descent.

After about 0.5 mile, you come to the first of two large onshore sea stacks. A hundred thousand years ago all but the tops of these stacks were under water. In the interim, the relentless movement of the San Andreas fault has pushed the land upward to its present level. The first, smaller stack has split in half, with a secondary trail right through its middle. This is a favorite spot for rock climbers. The second stack, about 0.8 mile along the trail, is the largest. Adventurous souls can cautiously scramble to its top for great views of the coastline. A large offshore sea stack here is called Gull Rock. Its solid-white color attests to its popularity as a nesting spot for cormorants and gulls.

You reach Shell Beach at just under 2 miles. If you're not ready to hike the entire trail, this is an excellent starting spot for a shorter hike in either direction. The trail crosses the west side of the parking lot near the toilets. The best wildflower displays occur south of Shell Beach, for unlike the trail to the north, cattle have not recently grazed here. About 0.5 mile beyond Shell

An optimistic spider waits for the big catch along the Kortum Trail south of Shell Beach.

Beach you descend a canyon into Furlong Gulch. You can take a short detour here to enjoy this somewhat isolated beach. Continuing southward, the formal trail ends at the north end of Wright's Beach, 1.3 miles from Shell Beach. The campground and day-use area are another 0.8 mile further along this sandy beach.

Vista Trail. This paved loop trail, located 4 miles north of Jenner, is accessible to the disabled. A good parking lot with a dozen spaces and a wooden outhouse is located well off the highway. The mile-long trail has great views of the coast and is a good place to watch for hawks. The entire trail extends across grassland and is reasonably level throughout. There are picnic tables at several spots along the way. At one point, a paved spur trail extends west to a wooden observation deck with a built-in bench. This is an ideal trail for families with small children.

Dr. David Joseph Memorial Pomo Canyon Trail. Follow a former Indian trading route through redwood forests and oak-covered hills on this trail that winds 3 miles inland. You can start from either the Pomo Canyon Environmental Campground or from Highway 1 directly across from the Shell Beach parking lot. This trail is more completely described in the section on Willow Creek below.

Willow Creek Area

The Willow Creek area lies in a broad canyon well back from the sea, separated from it by a line of hills. The weather here can be vastly different from the nearby coast. While the shoreline is blanketed in fog, Willow Creek may be bathed in sunlight and 15 degrees warmer. Two environmental campgrounds lie within the canyon. Willow Creek Environmental Camp sits on the Russian River, and Pomo Canyon Environmental Camp is three miles inland. The Dr. David Joseph Memorial Pomo Canyon Trail provides a vigorous hike through redwood forests and open grasslands along a former Indian trading route.

Directions

If you're coming from Jenner, take Highway 1 south. Immediately after crossing the Russian River highway bridge, turn east onto Willow Creek Road. From Bodega Bay, take Highway 1 north. Willow Creek Road is 0.6 mile past the turnoff for Goat Rock Beach. The Willow Creek Environmental Camp is on your left 0.5 mile from the highway, immediately past a house occupied by state park staff. Pomo Canyon Environmental Camp is down a dirt road on your right, 2.8 miles from the highway.

Willow Creek Environmental Camp

This is the only state park campground on the Russian River. Eleven primitive sites are available on a first-come-first-serve basis. You must self-register and pay your registration fee at the parking lot. The campground is open April 1 to November 30.

Like all environmental camps, Willow Creek is intended to provide a more secluded experience than possible at a developed campground. Sites are widely spaced and located for maximum privacy. Vehicles aren't allowed at the campsites, so you'll have to park in the lot and carry in your equipment. It's an easy walk of 90 to 770 yards, depending on your site. A pit toilet is located nearby.

Most of the sites sit in the trees surrounding a meadow. Site 10 is on the river bank. All sites have tables and all but site 5, which is located in an area of high fire danger, have metal fire rings. You must bring your own wood for fires, as you are not allowed to gather wood in the state park. Bring your own water, since there is none at the camp and Russian River water is unsuitable for drinking. Pets are not allowed at any environmental camp because wildlife will avoid areas frequented by domesticated animals.

Pomo Canyon Environmental Camp

Like Willow Creek, this campground is designed to give you a sense of solitude. The entrance road stretches 0.4 mile from Willow Creek Road through a grassy meadow to the parking area. The 20 campsites, including one accessible to the disabled, are situated in a redwood grove at the edge of the meadow within 0.3 mile of the parking lot. Once you have picked a site, you must self-register and pay the fee. You must carry your equipment from the lot to your campsite. Two pit toilets stand at the base of the trail, and there is a water spigot near the trailhead. No pets are allowed. The campground is open April 1 through November 30.

Hikers take in the sights along Pomo Canyon Trail. The town of Jenner lies in the distance.

The Dr. David Joseph Memorial Pomo Canyon Trail. This three-mile long trail climbs 700 feet through redwood forests and grassy hillsides before descending to Highway 1 across from Shell Beach. The trail begins at the west end of the Pomo Canyon Environmental Camp parking lot, where you must self-register and pay the day-use fee. (When the campground is closed in winter, you'll have to park at the gate and walk the level half-mile dirt road to the trailhead.)

The trail passes the outhouses on your left and through the environmental camp. Campsites lie on either side of the trail here. Notice the growth patterns of the redwoods in this grove. Many of the trees are growing in circular patterns around a central core. These are miniature fairy rings, which occur when a fallen tree regenerates from sprouts around the periphery of its stump. Redwoods are one of the few conifers that can develop from sprouts as well as seeds. These growth patterns confirm that this area was once logged; you can still see occasional stumps along the trail.

You continue a steady climb for 0.6 mile through the shaded forest. Watch for poison oak along the trailside. Finally, the ascent eases as you break out of the forest. The trail levels at about 0.8 mile. On your right is a rock outcrop with a short volunteer trail to its top. With its panoramic view out to Jenner and the northern coast, this is a good spot to stop for lunch or a snack.

Continuing along the main trail, you pass through several stands of fir, bay, and laurel, then emerge into a region of rolling grasslands. In the spring and summer, impressive wildflower displays can be seen here. On your left is an old fenceline, now nearly obscured by poison oak. At several points along the way you cross small wooden bridges over babbling brooks. On your right, you'll have excellent views of Jenner and the mouth of the Russian River.

Finally, after hiking just over 2 miles, you reach the top of the ridgeline. On a clear day, you are treated to a spectacular view of the southern coast all the way to Point Reyes. Notice the eroded rock outcroppings on your left, ancient sea stacks that have been lifted 600 feet by the relentless motion of the San Andreas Fault. Directly below, you have a good view of the offshore sea stack known as Gull Rock.

If you don't have a car waiting for you at Shell Beach, this might be a good place to turn back. The trail from here descends quickly to the sea through open grassland, so the last mile of the hike will add a 500-foot climb to your return trek.

For Further Reading

Grady, Rex, *Let Ocean Seethe and Terra Slide, a History of the Sonoma Coast and the State Park that Shares its Name*, Lilburne Press, Occidental, CA, 1998.

Day Use and Overnight Facilities—Sonoma Coast State Beach, California Department of Parks and Recreation, Feb 1986.

Lorentzen, Bob, *The Hiker's Hip Pocket Guide to Sonoma County*, Bored Feet Publications, Mendocino, CA, 1990.

Edwards, Don, *Making the Most of Sonoma County*, Valley of the Moon Press, Alameda, CA, 1986.

Kelleher, Brian T., *Drake's Bay: Unravelling California's Great Maritime Mystery*, Kelleher and Associates, Cupertino, CA, 1997.

History comes alive at the Fort Ross Living History Day each July.

3

Fort Ross State Historic Park

The weathered remains of California's first permanent coastal settlement north of San Francisco stand on a grassy bluff overlooking the ocean at Fort Ross. It was here in 1812 that Russian colonists established the southernmost outpost of their Pacific empire and very nearly changed the course of history. If not for a few twists of fate, what we now call Sonoma County might today be part of a Russian colony stretching from Alaska to the Golden Gate. But such was not to be, and the reconstructed fort now stands as a silent reminder of the harshness of pioneer life in a strange and isolated land.

The historic stockade is the centerpiece of 3303-acre Fort Ross State Historic Park. Here, you can explore the grounds and learn what life was like during the Russian era. Other points of interest include a visitor's center, a 20-site campground, day-use areas, ocean access, an underwater park, an orchard and cemetery dating back to Russian times, and the Stanley S. Spyra Memorial Redwood Grove. The San Andreas Fault also passes through the park. Although there are no designated hiking trails there are several informal paths and you are welcome to roam about the entire park. Remember to watch for poison oak when exploring the countryside!

Fast Facts

Internet home page: http://www.mcn.org/1/rrparks/parks/fortr.htm
Phone: 707-847-3286
Hours: Stockade and visitor's center open 10-4:30 daily. Park grounds open sunrise to sunset.
Interpretive Specialists: Interpretive specialists are on duty every day. They give tours of the fort several times during the day. Check at the visitor's center for current information.
Camping: Fort Ross Primitive Campground open April 1 through November 30 on a first-come-first-serve basis.
Best hiking trails: No designated trails, but you may explore throughout the park. Good hikes include the headlands northwest of the Visitor's Center and the logging road from the Stanley S. Spyra Memorial Grove to Kolmer Gulch. **Watch for poison oak!**

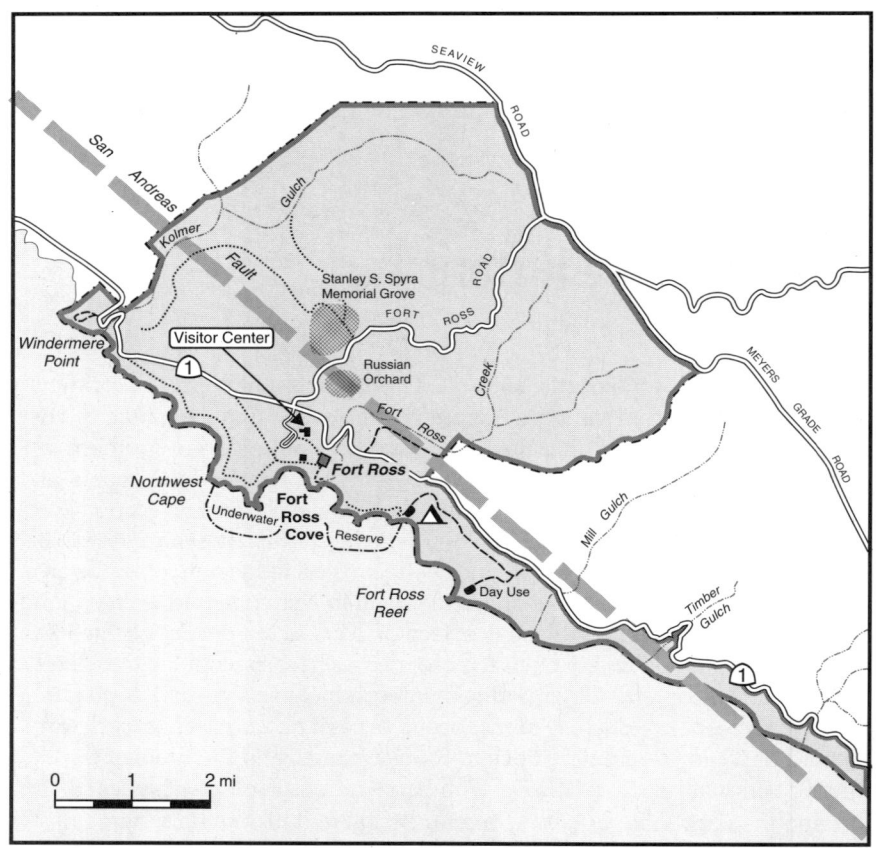

Fort Ross State Historic Park.

The park sponsors a Living History Day on the last Saturday of July each year. Volunteers dress in period costumes to depict a typical day during the Russian period of the early 19th century. Visitiors can watch a blacksmith at work, learn how to weave baskets, and listen to musicians playing traditional Russian music. Several times during the day, costumed participants recreate historic events such as visits from Spanish authorities or Yankee traders. A highlight of the day is the firing of the park's muzzle-loading cannons.

Archaeologists from the State and the University of California still excavate within the park. One major objective is to understand more about how Russian colonialism impacted the native Pomo people. Recent explorations have also uncovered, in the cove below the fort, the timbers of a shipway used to launch vessels constructed at the site. Remember that all archaeological relics within the park are protected and must not be disturbed.

Getting There

The park lies 11 miles north of the Russian River on State Highway 1. You come to the campground and day-use areas first, with the fort another 1.7 miles beyond.

The narrow, winding road out of Jenner quickly climbs as high as 600 feet above the sea, with sheer drops on your left. Passengers have excellent views of the rugged Sonoma Lost Coast along the way, but the driver will be too busy trying to stay on the road to appreciate them. Stop at any of the dirt pull-outs alongside the road to enjoy the scenery. Also be sure to watch out for cattle that occasionally meander onto the highway.

Natural Environment

The fort stands on open grassland along a coastal shelf. To its east lies a range of hills that alternate between redwood-forested canyons and exposed ridges. The San Andreas Fault runs along the base of these hills less than a mile from the fort. If you explore within the rift zone you will see ample evidence of geologic activity. Fault trenches and sag ponds are especially evident in the area near Kolmer Gulch.

The park harbors a rich variety of wildlife. Common animals include the black-tailed deer, brush rabbit, ground squirrel, raccoon, pocket gopher, and broad-handed mole. You may also be lucky enough to spot the elusive bobcat or gray fox. Mountain lions have occasionally been observed in the area, while black bear sitings are extremely rare. Numerous species of birds frequent the park, including hawks, ospreys, harriers, kestrels and an assortment of sea birds.

In Russian times, Fort Ross Cove was a bustle of industrial activity. Today, the fort stands guard over an isolated beach.

Supplemental Park Rules

The following rules supplement the general rules for California State Parks listed on Page 12.

Day Use Fees. You must pay a day-use fee if you drive through the main entrance to the fort or enter Fort Ross Reef. All vehicles visiting the fort must park in the main lot unless they have a handicap placard. You may drive to the fort, to the Call Ranch picnic area, or down to Fort Ross Cove to unload passengers and supplies but you must immediately return to the main parking lot.

Camping. The only campground in the park is at Fort Ross Reef. It is open from April 1 through November 30. Camping is allowed only in designated campsites. Campsites are available on a first-come-first-served basis and are not on the state park reservation system.

Animals. All animals within the park are protected from molestation and injury. State Fish and Game regulations govern all activities above mean high tide. Within this authority, tidepool creatures are also protected. Separate Federal laws protect marine mammals (see Page 14.)

Collecting. All living and non-living things are protected within the park and may not be collected. You must obtain a permit from the district superintendent for any exceptions. Geological and archaeological features are also protected.

Pets. Animals must be kept leashed and under control at all times. Pets are permitted only on the north side of the main parking lot. They are not allowed in the visitor's center, the fort, or on any trail.

Horses: Although you may ride horses on any of the park's trails and fire roads, there are no accommodations in the park for horse trailers. You must ride your horse in from outside the park.

Off-Highway Vehicles. No vehicles, including mountain bikes, are allowed off road in the park.

The weather here is typical of the Sonoma Coast. Summer highs are commonly 60-80 degrees F, cooling into the 50's at night. The habitual morning fogs and afternoon winds make it seem colder. Spring, with its beautiful wildflower displays and less frequent fog, is an especially good time to visit.

History

Humans have lived in the Fort Ross area for at least 7000 years. At the time of European contact in the 1700's, the region around Fort Ross was the domain of the Pomo Indians. The Pomo were not a tribe in the classical sense, nor were they nomadic like the Indians of the Great Plains. Rather, they lived in localized bands consisting of no more than a few hundred people. Each band had its own territory that was fiercely protected. Dozens of bands lived in relative harmony throughout what is now Sonoma County. Those in the Fort Ross area were known as the Kashaya ("agile people") Pomo.

Amid such fertile surroundings, the Kashaya had no need for agriculture. From the shore, they harvested abalone, mussels, fish, crabs, and marine mammals. From the inland areas they hunted deer, elk, and numerous smaller animals. They also gathered a bountiful supply of nuts, berries, seeds, greens, and vegetables. During the summer months, they lived along the coast, while in the fall, they moved inland to warmer, more protected settlements.

The Russians were drawn to this region in search of sea otter pelts for their lucrative fur trade with Europe and the Orient. Their eastward expansion through Siberia and beyond paralleled America's push westward. As the English were settling New England, Russian fur hunters reached the Pacific Ocean. They began exploring the Aleutians in the middle of the 18th century and by 1784 had established outposts all the way to Kodiak Island.

In 1799, based on glowing reports from the east, Czar Paul granted the Russian-American Company exclusive rights to hunt furs from Siberia to the Alaskan mainland. Facing high expectations, Aleksandr Baranov, the company manager at the Alaskan outpost of Fort Alexander, struggled to make the venture as profitable as his superiors had led the Czar to believe. The Alaskan climate was harsh, and many of the settlers were unwilling serfs. Most did not take even the most elementary sanitary precautions, so sickness was a constant problem.

For years, Baranov had tried to improve conditions at the Alaskan colony. He instituted military discipline and improved relations with the local natives. In 1799 he led an expedition to establish a new outpost at Sitka. Morale gradually improved, but the colonists were poor farmers so the food shortages continued. To make matters worse, the Sitka outpost was nearly wiped out in an 1802 Indian uprising.

Wooden crosses mark the Russian cemetery on a hill overlooking the fort.

With a cloud of smoke and a deafening roar, volunteers fire one of the fort's cannons during Living History Day.

In 1805, the head of the Russian-American Company, Nikolai Petrovich Rezanov, sailed into Sitka. Although the 42-year-old Russian nobleman had been a company official for ten years, he had never before visited the Alaskan colonies. The dilapidated shacks and starving colonists he found were a stark contrast to the prosperous settlements described in dispatches. Baranov offered to resign on the spot, but Rezanov would have none of it. The two discussed the situation and soon agreed that the answer to their problems lay in southern expansion.

Rezanov led an expedition to San Francisco in the spring of 1806. His scurvy-ridden crew were in desparate straits as they sailed through the Golden Gate on April 5. But the erudite Rezanov soon won over the suspicious Spaniards. He entered into a profitable trade arrangement in which the Russians received much-needed food in exchange for fine silks and furs.

Rezanov also courted María de la Conceptión Argüello y Moraga, the beautiful and charming 16-year-old daughter of the military commander. The two became engaged on condition that Rezanov, a Russian Orthodox, first return to St. Petersburg and receive papal dispensation to marry the Catholic María.

Rezanov left for Sitka on May 21, promising María he would return within two years. By February, 1807, he was in Siberia, ill with malaria but determined to reach St. Petersburg as quickly as possible. But while riding hard across the icy plains, he was killed when he fainted and fell from his horse. Years passed before María learned of Rezanov's death. Never marrying, she became a nun and lived in solitude until her death in 1857. Her plight was immortalized in a famous Bret Harte poem.

Had Rezanov returned to wed María, it could have altered the course of California history. United by marriage, Spain and Russia would have become formidable trading partners with an iron hold on the land. But with his death, so too died the dreams of a Russo-Spanish alliance, and the Spaniards returned once again to viewing the Russians as unwanted foreigners.

On his return to Sitka, Rezanov had urged Baranov to establish a hunting and farming colony north of San Francisco. So in 1808, Baranov sent an expedition under the command of Ivan Kuskov to search out a site. The peg-legged Kuskov was one of the few men in the colony with the imagination and initiative to make the venture successful.

Forty Russians and 150 Native Alaskan Koniag and Aleut hunters landed in Bodega Bay (called Rumiantzov Bay by the Russians) in late December. The native Alaskan hunters, sailing small kayaks called *baidarkas*, were phenomenally successful in the hunt. By the time the expedition returned to Sitka the following October, they had collected over 2000 seal and otter furs.

Kuskov led another expedition to Bodega Bay in 1811. They explored the countryside and traveled 50 miles up the Russian River, which they named the *Slavianka* ("Charming Little Slav Girl"). By now the Spanish were alerted to the Russian presence, but their small detachment was too weak to evict them. Once again, the Russians returned to Sitka with a bountiful harvest of furs.

These expeditions were so successful that Baranov sent Kuskov, along with 25 Russians and 80 Native Alaskans, back again to found a permanent colony in 1812. Kuskov decided that Bodega Bay was too close to San Francisco to be adequately defended, so he selected a spot about 18 miles farther north. The site had better soil, water, and pasture land, although its small cove was unable to accommodate large ships. Kuskov negotiated with the local Kashaya Pomo to purchase the land. According to accounts of the time, the purchase price was "three blankets, three pairs of breeches, two axes, three hoes, and some beads." Hardly a princely sum, but it was the only known instance during California's Spanish period in which land was actually purchased from the natives rather than simply taken from them.

Uncertain of Spanish intentions, the colonists immediately erected the thirteen-foot-high stockade walls. Around the fort and in the blockhouses at the north and south corners, as many as 40 cannons—some captured during Napoleon's retreat from Moscow—guarded the surroundings. Other buildings eventually erected within the fort included barracks, storehouses, manager's house, and chapel. Most of the Russian colonists lived in houses outside the fort, along with the Aleuts and a village of Kashaya Pomo. Bodega Bay, with its better harbor, remained the colony's principal port.

Archaeologists from the University of California slowly excavate the foundation of a Russian building near Fort Ross Cove.

The settlement, named *Rossiya* after the ancient name for the Russian homeland, was dedicated on August 13, 1812. To the Spanish, it became known as "Fuerto de los Rusos," while the Americans simply called it "Fort Ross."

Officially, both Spain and the United States viewed the Russian outpost with alarm. President James Monroe even issued his famous Monroe Doctrine in part to warn the Russians to depart. But the local Spaniards were generally willing to look the other way. San Francisco was a lonely and isolated outpost, so the prospect of meeting interesting foreigners was appealing. Clandestine trading was common, and in later years, Mexican officials were sometimes invited to ceremonial events.

The abundance of nearby timber encouraged company officials to set up a shipyard in the cove below the fort, the first in California. Over a period of eight years four large brigs and several smaller ships were built and launched from the site. (Hardly master shipbuilders, their vessels rotted and sank with alarming regularity.)

The fort also gave Russian scientists a base to study the flora and fauna of the north coast. On one visit, the Russian naturalist Adelbert von Chamisso collected samples of the California poppy. He gave it the scientific name, *Eschscholtzia Californica*, after his friend and fellow traveler, the entomologist Johan Eschscholtz. Later, the governor-general of Russian America, Baron Ferdinand von Wrangell, led a major anthropological study of Indian tribes in the Sonoma County area.

The fear and strife so common elsewhere between Indians and Europeans did not exist at Fort Ross because the Russians treated the Kashaya with relative fairness. Indians received reasonable wages for their work, as well as lodging and clothing. They were not held against their will, and many Russian and Alaskan men married Kashaya women, creating a unique tricultural community.

In the early years, the fur harvest was profitable, but by the 1820's over-harvesting had decimated the sea otter population. So the colony turned to agriculture and livestock-raising as the dominant occupations. The old Russian orchard on the east side of Highway 1 survives as a remnant of this effort. But the colony was never successful enough to significantly help the Alaskan outposts. The colonists considered themselves hunters rather than farmers, so they never spent the time necessary to learn the finer points of farming. That, coupled with problems of gophers, mice, and coastal fog, doomed their efforts. Debts mounted year by year, and eventually the Russians were forced to withdraw. They unsuccessfully tried to sell the fort in turn to the Hudson's Bay Company, Mariano Vallejo, and the Mexican government. Finally, in 1841, they reached an agreement with John Sutter, of Sutter's Fort along the American River. After the purchase, he dismantled many of the buildings and used them to help found the town of Sacramento.

After the Russians departed, Mexico rejected Sutter's claim to the land and instead granted title to Manuel Torres. The fort changed hands several times in subsequent years until 1873, when it was purchased by George W. Call. Besides raising cattle, he also grew fruits and vegetables and conducted a profitable lumber-harvesting operation at the site. The Call family owned the land as part of a 15,000 acre ranch until 1903, when they sold the fort and 3 acres of land to the California Historical Landmarks Committee. By the time it was turned over to the State of California in March, 1906, much of the original construction had deteriorated or been removed. Less than a month later, the fort was ravaged by the great San Francisco earthquake. Over the years, the state has carried out extensive restoration work and continued to add acreage, so that today the fort is similar to its appearance in the Russian period.

Stockade and Surroundings

Driving north on Highway 1, you'll catch your first glimpse of the fort walls while still two miles away. Unlike many historic sites now enveloped by commercial development, Fort Ross sits in an environment largely unchanged from Ivan Kuskov's day. In fact, thanks in part to careful preservation efforts by a number of people, the region is less developed now than it was during the Russian period.

As you drive past the fort, look for a driveway on your left leading to the stockade. This was the original route of Highway 1, which went right through the center of the compound until 1972, when it was relocated to its present route. You'll find the park's main entrance a short distance north, opposite the junction with Fort Ross Road. Stop at the kiosk to pay your entrance fee, then continue to the large parking lot at the visitor's center. Here, you'll find an easy path to the fort. Along the trail, you'll pass numerous gar-

During the school year, Fort Ross serves as an overnight outdoor education site for elementary school children. These garden plots were planted by children serving in the role of agronomists.

den plots planted by elementary school children as part of an overnight outdoor education experience.

Many visitors seem to think they are done once they've toured the stockade. Don't fall into this trap; there is much to see beyond the fort walls. Several points of interest are easily accessible from the main parking lot.

Stockade

Few people realize that most of what you now see of the stockade is a reconstruction of the original. One exception is the Rotchev House, built in 1836. Only a few of the other structures that once stood here have been restored. The following structures now stand within the stockade walls.

Kuskov House. This two-story building was the original commandant's house. The upper story contained the living quarters while the lower story contained the armory and storerooms. After Alexander Rotchev moved the commandant's residence to new quarters, the Kuskov House may have provided lodging for scientists and other distinguished visitors who stayed for long periods.

Chapel.

Chapel. Nothing symbolizes the resilience of Fort Ross more that its simple wooden chapel. Built around 1824, it was the first Russian Orthodox church in North America outside of Alaska. The hardy structure survived the ravages of time until 1906, when it collapsed during the great San Francisco

Kuskov House.

earthquake. It could easily have been written off as irretrievably lost, but citizens' groups from around the state persevered. Finally in 1916 they convinced the state legislature to appropriate $3,000 for reconstruction. George Call's son, Carlos, supervised the work. Fortunately, the roof, cupola, and bell tower were still intact, so most of the effort involved constructing new walls and foundations.

This reconstruction was not completely faithful to the original. To strengthen the walls, extra beams were added, so the number of side windows had to increase from three to four. There were also errors in the alignment with the stockade walls. Not until 1956 were these flaws corrected during a second restoration supervised by the park's historian, John C. McKenzie. His careful research and meticulous attention to detail were essential in assuring historical accuracy.

Another potentially fatal disaster occurred on October 5, 1970, when a fire of unknown origin burned the little chapel to the ground. Once again, supporters rallied to raise the funds to rebuild it. This time the reconstruction accurately duplicated the Russian original, including faithful reproductions of materials and construction techniques.

South Blockhouse. Part of the original stockade, the south blockhouse has eight sides. It guards the southeast and southwest walls, and its cannon

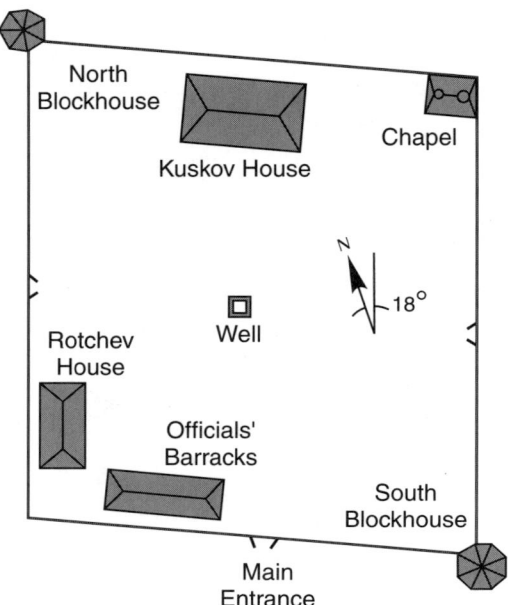

Layout of existing stockade.

could fire on ships at sea. It was partially rebuilt during the chapel's 1917 restoration and was completed by McKenzie in 1956-57.

Officials' Barracks. This structure, complete with kitchen and office, provided living accommodations for Russian officials and routine visitors. It also included storerooms, a jail, and workshops. During the late 1800's, its south end served as a saloon. The original timbers from the barracks were removed in 1917 and used to help reconstruct the chapel.

Rotchev House. Until Alexander Rotchev took over as the fort's final commander in 1836, no Russian women had lived in the commandant's house since Ivan Kuskov's departure 15 years earlier. When Rotchev and his wife, the former Princess Helena Gagarina, arrived they immediately brought a new level of sophostication to the colony. But Helena was aghast at the idea of living in the Kuskov House above an arsenal full of explosive gunpowder. She immediately demanded new living quarters. The new residence, known as the Rotchev House, was located as far from the arsenal as possible.

After the Russians left, various owners made modifications to the house. William Benitz enlarged it for his family in 1847. He extended the building on the north and added a partial second story on the south. The Call family used it as a residence until completing their ranch house in 1878. It subsequently became a hotel before falling into disrepair. Restoration work began in 1926 and continued off and on for another half-century. The non-Russian additions were removed and various other repairs were carried out to restore its original appearance. Damaged by a fire in 1972, it was refurbished and opened to the public in 1974. The Rotchev House is the only surviving original structure and is the oldest wooden building west of the Mississippi.

North Blockhouse. Unlike the south blockhouse, the north tower has only seven sides. It commands an unobstructed view over the northeast and northwest walls. After lying in disrepair for a number of years, it was ultimately rebuilt in 1948.

Well. At the center of the stockade lies a well capable of providing water even during siege. Opinions differ as to whether it or Fort Ross Creek was the colony's primary water source in routine times. The well has been shown to be one of the few reliable year-round water sources in the vicinity.

During the Russian period several additional buildings existed within the compound. These included a two-story fur barn north of the Rotchev House, a barracks for unmarried employees south of the chapel, and a warehouse/kitchen near the south blockhouse. These structures have all long since disappeared, though park officials hope to eventually reconstruct some of them.

Visitor's Center

Be sure to stop in at the visitor's center before continuing on to the stockade. You'll find interpretive displays of the fort's history, a theater showing

Visitor's center.

Call Ranch House.

slide and video presentations related to the park, and a wide range of books and postcards for sale. The bookstore is staffed by volunteers from the Fort Ross Interpretive Association, and proceeds are used to help fund research grants, maintenance of the old Russian orchard, restoration of buildings, and the Environmental Living Program for elementary school children.

Call Ranch House and Picnic Area

After touring the stockade, exit through the southwest gate, opposite the Kuskov House. Follow the paved road as it bears right. For many years, this was the route of Highway 1. The wooden two-story ranch house stands on your right a few hundred feet from the fort. This was the house George W. Call built for his family in 1878. He also started a weather station here that is still in use today, making it the oldest weather station on the west coast. You'll have to appreciate the view from outside, as the house is not open to the public.

Behind the house you can see a wooden barn, another relic from the Call period. Just past the ranch house is a picnic area with tables. From here, you can either turn right and follow a foot path through a picturesque eucalyptus and Monterey cypress grove back to the visitor's center or continue along the road back to the west end of the parking lot.

Fort Ross Cove

From the stockade's main gate, take the path south toward the sea. Follow it down the side of the cove to an excellent sandy beach with picnic tables. During the Russian period this was the industrial center of the colony. It was here that the Russians set up California's first shipyard, as well as a tannery and blacksmith's shop. The remains of a wooden shipway and ship-building materials were excavated here in 1996-97 after being exposed by a winter storm.

Underwater Park

The waters from Northwest Cape to Fort Ross Reef have been designated as an underwater park. Unlike the marine reserve at Salt Point State Park, you may still fish and dive for abalone here. However, as a park, it is afforded somewhat more protection that the surrounding waters.

Russian Cemetery

The old Russian cemetery stands on a grassy knoll across Fort Ross Creek from the stockade. The easiest access is from Highway 1 southeast of the fort. Park at a small gravel pull-out near milepost 32.18, directly across from a gated dirt access road. Walk through an opening in the fence to the cemetery. The Russian Orthodox crosses marking the known burial sites are recent additions to replace the long-decayed original markers.

Along Fort Ross Road

Russian Orchard

You reach the orchard by driving along Fort Ross Road, which intersects Highway 1 directly across from the main park entrance. The orchard lies 0.5 mile up the road on the right. It is protected by a chain-link fence, so you will have to observe it from a distance.

Several trees in the old orchard survive from Russian times.

The first trees to be planted were peaches brought from San Francisco in 1814. Eventually, plantings were expanded to include hundreds of apple, cherry, and pear trees. The orchard continues in service today, with several of the original trees remaining. The Russians also planted grapes here, thereby earning the distinction of being Sonoma County's first vintners. Their lack of success would hardly have foretold the region's future prospects as a center for fine wine.

Stanley S. Spyra Memorial Grove

This stately redwood grove lies nearly opposite the old orchard. The area was clear-cut by the Russians, so the trees here are now the world's oldest second-growth coast redwoods. A number of their trunks were broken dur-

ing the 1906 earthquake when the ground moved more than seven feet in
less than a minute.

San Andreas Fault

The San Andreas rift zone passes just east of the stockade, running
through the orchard and redwood grove. Ground movement over many centuries has caused portions of both Fort Ross Creek and Kolmer Gulch to
turn parallel to the fault.

Kolmer Gulch Trail

You can see evidence of the fault by hiking an old logging road from the
Stanley S. Spyra Memorial Grove to Kolmer Gulch. Park at the grove entrance across from the Russian orchard, being careful not to block the gate.
As you walk the path, notice the fault trench to your left. You soon come to
a large, reed-filled sag pond on your right, surrounded by horsetail ferns.
Sag ponds occur when the ground sinks along the fault, forming an elongated depression that captures rainwater. Smaller ponds dry up by late summer, but this one is large enough to stay wet year round.

After a few hundred yards the trail forks. Take the path to your left,
marked "Lower Kolmer Gulch." You quickly emerge from the forest into
open grassland. As you crest a slight rise, look down to your left to see another, smaller sag pond. The road then makes a gentle "S" curve, sweeping
left and then right through rolling grasslands. You then re-enter forest for the
remainder of your hike. The open forest here was logged by the Call family.
You can still see frequent stumps, many now over 100 years old. In the
spring and early summer a profusion of wildflowers bloom along the trail.
The foxglove, with its columns of pink bell-shaped flowers, is especially striking.

The trail descends gradually at first, but about a mile into the hike it
curves left and becomes somewhat steeper. You are well away from traffic
noise here, so you may want to settle in for awhile and listen to the sounds
of the forest. In another half mile you reach a fork in the trail. The logging
road turns right and descends into Kolmer Gulch. It soon becomes overgrown, so rather than following the road, take the left fork, a single-track trail
you might not initially notice.

You can allegedly hike all the way down to Highway 1, though I haven't
gone that far. The trail becomes steeper near the end, so unless you have a
vehicle waiting for you at the highway, it might be wise to turn around at
this point.

Returning to the trail fork, you may want to explore the Upper Kolmer
Gulch section of the trail. You'll see several fault trenches and sag ponds as
you descend gradually to the creek. Kolmer Gulch Camp, about 0.8 mile
along the road, is the site of an old logging camp and was used by the Call

family for barbeques. There are picnic tables, barbeque pits, and running water here. It's a great spot for a picnic, but no overnight camping is allowed.

North Headlands

If your tastes run to hiking, wildlife observation, and coastal exploration, this is the area for you. You can start either at the fort's main parking lot or at Windermere Point to explore the various trails that stretch out over the headlands. Windermere Point also provides ocean access.

Hiking the North Headlands

Although there are no designated trails, a path of sorts traverses the headlands from Northwest Cape to Highway 1 near Windermere Point. Start from the southwest end of the main parking lot, where a dirt road departs for the fort. After a short distance the road curves left to join the old route of Highway 1. The old highway also extends to your right, but continue on toward the fort. Just before the speed limit sign you come to a single-track trail on your right heading toward a fence. Follow this trail through the fence and up a saddle through a rocky outcrop. You see various paths departing in either direction. You're welcome to explore any of them, but the described route continues southwest across open grassland toward the cape.

The trail becomes hard to follow, but it really doesn't matter because you have an unobstructed view over the entire route. Study the path shown on the Fort Ross map, in general staying near the edge of the bluffs without get-

Fog and wind don't deter these picnickers from enjoying the headlands.

ting close enough to fall off. You have excellent views of the fort and cove as you head toward the cape.

Northwest Cape is covered in yellow bush lupine, with sticky monkeyflower and coast buckwheat growing along the bluff rims. Continue on around the cape, turning northward. You cross various gullies and seasonal streams along this stretch. You also may have to navigate around idly grazing cattle, for the Parks Department leases this land to local ranchers.

There are several steep volunteer trails to the beach along this section, but they are dangerous and not worth the risk. You can continue all the way to Highway 1 after a hike of about 1.5 miles, or you can turn east and return along the old highway at any of several points for a shorter hike.

Windermere Point

This jutting point at the north end of the park is named after a ship that wrecked here in 1883. Today, it provides ocean access to divers and fishermen. A rough dirt loop road departs west from the highway at the north side of the hairpin curve through Kolmer Gulch.

Reef Campground and Day-Use Areas

The only camping allowed in the park is at Fort Ross Reef Campground, set in a protected canyon southeast of the stockade. There are also two day-use areas here. Fees are charged both for camping and for day use.

Campground

The campground entrance is located along Highway 1 near milepost 31.37. Register at the kiosk, then continue along the road to the campsites. Open from April 1 to November 30, the campground contains 20 sites available on a first-come-first-served basis. Because of very limited turning space, the campground cannot accommodate large recreational vehicles. Each campsite includes a picnic table and fire ring. Outhouses with sinks

Fort Ross Reef Campground.

and flush toilets are nearby, as are water faucets, but there are no showers. During periods of high fire danger, campfires are not allowed, so be sure to check posted signs.

Day-Use Areas

The northern day-use area lies at the end of the road past the campground. A relatively easy path at the south end of the parking lot leads to a coarse gravel beach. Another, longer path on the north end leads to a rocky shoreline. The northern trail is more difficult; the last 20 feet involve scrambling over boulders down a rocky gully to the sea.

The road to the southern day-use area lies immediately left of the entrance kiosk. After paying your fee, take the narrow dirt road 0.25 mile to the grassy parking area. A poor dirt trail leads 120 feet down to a coarse gravel beach whose upper reaches are covered in driftwood. The trail is steep and narrow over loose dirt, so use extreme caution during the descent.

The day-use areas are popular spots for abalone diving and tidepooling. (A valid California fishing license is required for any person 16 years of age and older.) The reef is also a favorite spot for surfers willing to brave the cold Pacific waters and rocky shoreline.

Fort Ross Reef Trail

An easy trail leads from the northern day-use area to the bluff overlooking Fort Ross Cove. It departs from the northwest end of the parking lot and climbs up the side of the bluff. When you reach the crest, you look out over the headlands to the fort half a mile away. The view here looks very much as it must have appeared during the Russian period.

The level but somewhat vague trail then follows the cliffline, where such wildflowers as purple bush lupine, Indian paintbrush, and cow parsnip bloom in spring. When you reach the cove overlook, look around and try to picture what it must have been like during Russian times, when it was bustling with industrial activity. From here, you may be tempted to hike down a steep, narrow path to the beach. This descent is not for the faint of heart, for the path clings precariously to the side of the sheer bluff. Be extremely cautious if you decide to take this trail, as a fall here would result in serious injury or even death. You are especially advised not to descend if you have children. It is much easier and safer to reach the beach from the wide trail on the stockade side.

For Further Reading

O'Brien, Bickford, ed., *Fort Ross: Indians, Russians, Americans*, Fort Ross Interpretive Association, Jenner, CA, 1980.

Roske, Ralph J., *Everyman's Eden—a History of California*, The MacMillan Co, New York, 1968.

Wilson, Simone, *Sonoma County, The River of Time*, Windsor Publications, Inc., Chatsworth, CA, 1990.

Lorentzen, Bob, *The Hiker's Hip Pocket Guide to Sonoma County*, Bored Feet Publications, Mendocino, CA, 1990.

Edwards, Don, *Making the Most of Sonoma County*, Valley of the Moon Press, Alameda, CA, 1986.

Sculptured sandstone south of Gerstle Cove.

4

Salt Point State Park
Kruse Rhododendron State Reserve

The scenic beauty of the Sonoma coast is nowhere more evident than at Salt Point State Park. Here, you'll find rugged cliffs with dramatic ocean views. You'll also see magnificent natural sandstone sculptures, products of the relentless action of wind and waves. On the hills behind the sea you'll walk through quiet forests and grassy meadows, while at the top of the coastal ridge, you'll discover a rare pygmy forest of stunted cypress, pine, and redwood. Twenty miles of trails let you explore the varied terrain and plant communities within the park. Many trails are open to horses, and, from April through October, to well-conditioned mountain bikers as well.

Salt Point's attractions do not stop at the shoreline. It is a favorite destination for abalone divers, who are the leading users of the park. Divers are also drawn to Gerstle Cove Underwater Reserve, one of the first underwater parks in California. Even if you are not a diver you can still experience the wonders of the sea by exploring tidepools at low tide.

Fast Facts

Internet home page: http://www.mcn.org/1/rrparks/parks/saltp.htm
Park headquarters: Woodside Campground
Phone: 707-847-3221
Ocean conditions: 707-847-3222
Visitor's Center: Open weekends 10:00 am to 4:00 pm, 4/1-11/30.
Camping:
Woodside: open all year, reservations recommended 3/1-11/30.
Woodside walk-in: open 4/1-11/30, weather permitting. Reservations recommended. Sites are 0.5 mi hike.
Woodside hiker/biker: first come-first serve, no vehicles allowed.
Gerstle Cove: open all year, reservations recommended 3/1-11/30.
Best hiking trails: Salt Point Headlands Trail, Bluff Trail, North Trail, Central Trail, South Trail, Stump Beach Trail.

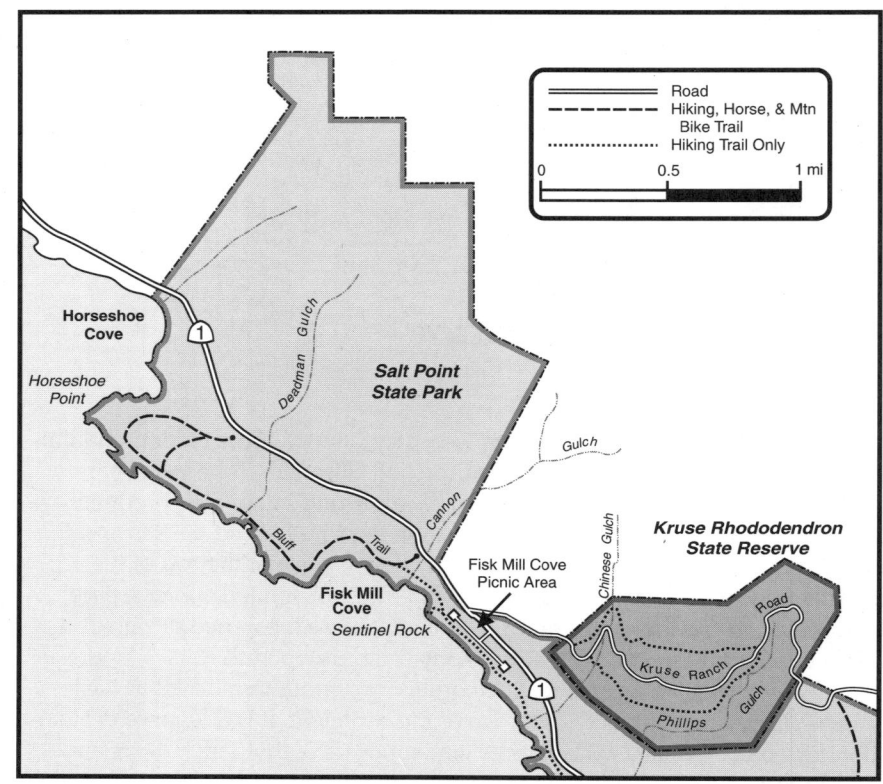

Salt Point State Park northern region and Kruse Rhododendron State Reserve.

Directly adjacent to Salt Point lies Kruse Rhododendron State Reserve. Five miles of hiking trails lead through forested canyons where, in the spring, you'll see striking displays of flowering rhododendrons.

Getting There

Salt Point State Park lies along State Highway 1, 20 miles north of Jenner and 8 miles north of Fort Ross. The road is narrow and winding, so figure on at least a 40-minute drive once you leave Jenner. Kruse Rhododendron State Reserve lies along Kruse Ranch Road, 0.5 mile east of its intersection with Highway 1. This is also the way to several trailheads on the east side of Salt Point.

Natural Environment

The park consists of three major environments: coniferous forest, grassland, and brush. Just over three-quarters of the park is covered by forests of

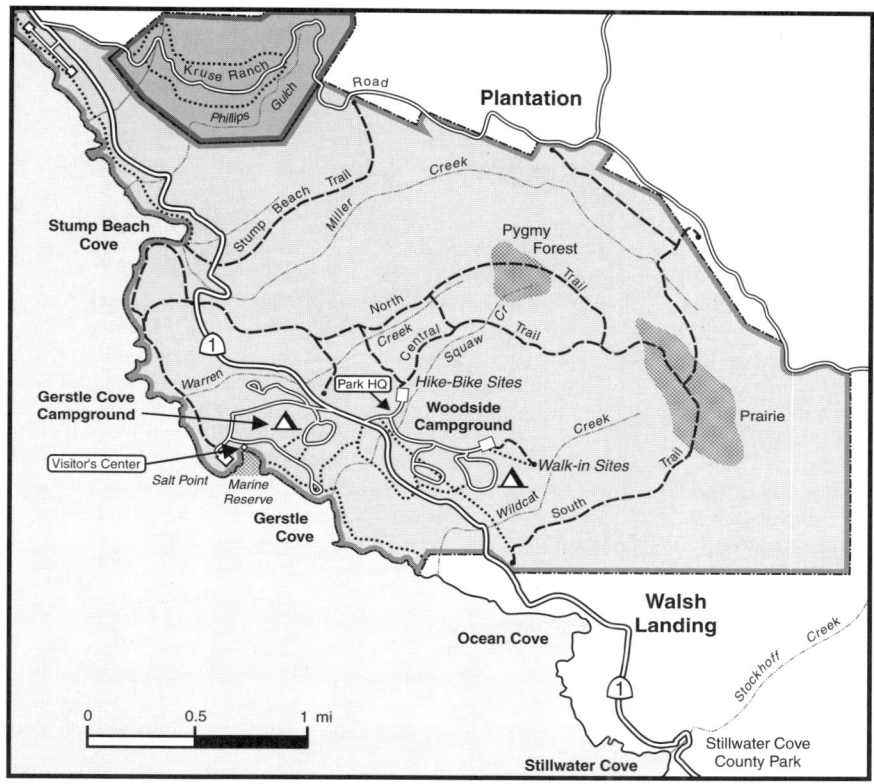

Salt Point State Park southern region.

coast redwood, Douglas fir, Bishop pine, tanoak, and madrone. Less than 10 percent is covered in brush, with the remainder consisting of grasslands. The pygmy forest is the result of unusually poor soil conditions in the region of the San Andreas Fault.

In many places, the forest extends right to the ocean. Elsewhere, a buffer of brush and grassland lies between the forest and sea. Here, you'll find such shrubs as sagebrush, lupine, Indian paintbrush, seaside daisy, and cow parsnip, as well as various native perennial and introduced annual grasses. Wildflowers can be spectacular in the spring.

Kruse Rhododendron State Reserve is a mixed forest of tanoak, fir, and second-growth redwood. Many years ago, fire swept through the area, clearing much of the forest and allowing the rhododendrons to flourish. Over time, the forest has started to return—the tanoaks first, followed by Douglas firs, grand firs, and eventually redwoods. As the conifers take over, the rhododendrons are being squeezed out. The Department of Parks and Recrea-

Supplemental Park Rules

The following rules supplement the general rules for California State Parks listed on Page 12.

Day Use Fees. Day use fees are collected at the Woodside entrance, at the Gerstle Cove entrance, and at Fisk Mill Cove.

Camping. Camping is allowed only in designated campsites. There are developed campgrounds at Woodside and at Gerstle Cove, open Mar 1 through Nov 30. Sites may be reserved by calling the toll-free reservation number at 800-444-7275. Gerstle Cove also has an overflow area for self-contained motorhomes and trailers when all campsites are full. A walk-in camp for tents only (sites 0.5 mile from the parking area) is located at the Woodside Campground. Reservations may be made through the toll-free reservation number. In addition, Woodside has a small hiker/biker campground, not on the reservation system, for individuals without automobiles.

Animals. All animals within the park are protected from molestation and injury. State Fish and Game regulations govern all activities above mean high tide. Within this authority, tidepool creatures are also protected. Separate Federal laws protect marine mammals (see Page 14.) Review the section on abalone hunting in this chapter and consult current fishing regulations before taking abalone along this coast.

Collecting. All living and non-living things are protected within the park and may not be collected. You must obtain a permit from the district superintendent for any exceptions. Geological and archaeological features are also protected. Mushroom collecting is currently permitted only in Salt Point State Park. Review the information in this chapter and consult with park staff before taking any mushrooms from the park.

Dogs. Dogs must be kept on a leash at all times and are permitted only in the developed areas of Woodside, Gerstle Cove, and Fisk Mill Cove. Dogs are not permitted on trails.

Horses: Horses are allowed on Stump Beach Trail, North Trail, Central Trail, South Trail, and Bluff Trail north of Cannon Gulch. Consult with rangers for current regulations.

Mountain Bikes. Mountain bikes are permitted on Stump Beach Trail, North Trail, Central Trail, South Trail, and Bluff Trail north of Cannon Gulch from April through October only. Because of their impact on trail conditions, mountain bikes are not permitted on trails immediately after rains when the trails are still muddy. Consult with rangers for current regulations.

tion thinned out the tanoak trees in the early 1980's as part of their goal of maintaining the beautiful rhododendron displays.

Tafoni. Salt Point is world-renown for its dramatic sandstone formations. A varied assortment of concretions, pedestals, and hollows are the result of fifty million years of wind and water erosion. These elaborate sandstone shapes occur because when the rock originally formed, mineral solutions seeped into the solidifying mass to produce localized regions harder than the surrounding rock. Once exposed, the softer sandstone was eroded by wind

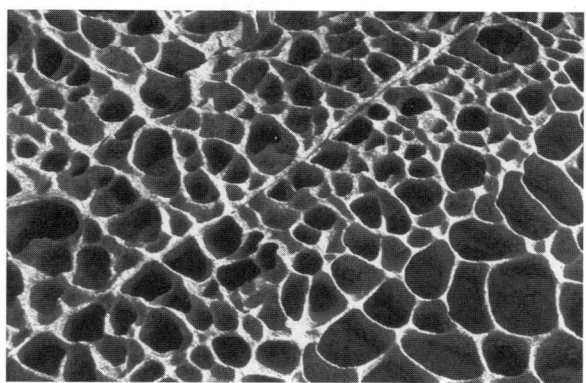

Detail of tafoni sandstone. The intricate structure is probably the result of mineral solutions that seeped along cracks in the dry sand, forming local regions harder than their surroundings.

and water, leaving the harder rock behind. Particularly intriguing are the strange, honeycombed structures known as *tafoni*. These waffled shapes were probably formed as the mineral solutions seeped along a series of fractures in the sand comparable to those found on dried mudflats.

Wildlife. Salt Point is home to an abundance of wildlife. Common mammals include the black tailed deer, raccoon, coyote, bobcat, gray fox, striped skunk, badger, squirrel, chipmunk, and field mouse. Wild pigs descended from domestic animals are also common. And like much of the west, mountain lions are making a comeback, with several sitings reported each year. Black bear are very rare, with only two recorded sitings over an eight year period. Raccoon and deer are common problems in the campgrounds, so always keep your food protected.

Birds include pelicans, ospreys, and a variety of shore and water-oriented species. You can also watch for gray whales from several spots in the park; Sentinel Rock is an especially good choice.

Abalone Hunting

There seem to be only two opinions of abalone. You either love it or you hate it. Those who love it flock to the Sonoma coast each year to hunt this tasty gastropod. Salt Point is a favorite destination for dedicated divers, but it is also a dangerous area that demands respect. Several people die every year because they overestimate their abilities or underestimate the power of the surf. Before diving, be sure to call the Salt Point dive phone at 707-847-3222 for current ocean and dive conditions. The recording is updated each morning around 8:30 am and again if conditions change significantly. Also review the rules of ocean safety on Page 15.

Abalone live from the intertidal zone down to depths of several hundred feet, depending on water temperature. They are often found on rocks and crevices exposed to heavy surf. In northern California it is illegal to use scuba equipment while collecting; you must free dive. The season runs from April through June, then again from August through November.

When you spot your victim, you must pry it loose with a legal-size abalone iron. You are not allowed to use knives, screwdrivers, or sharp instruments. For red abalone the shell must be at least 7 inches across at its greatest diameter, and you can collect a maximum of 4 abalone per day. You must immediately return an undersize specimen to the same rock you found it. You also must keep any legal size abalone you detach; you can't exchange a smaller one for a larger one you find later. Abalone must be kept in their shells until you are ready to eat them so that game wardens can confirm your catch meets the minimum size requirement.

Wardens have stepped up their patrols in recent years because of several well-publicized cases in which tons of abalone were illegally harvested for commercial use. Violators are aggressively prosecuted; heavy fines are routine and prison terms have even been meted out to the worst offenders. Wardens frequently set up inspection checkpoints along Highway 1, so be sure your catch is legal and you have a valid California fishing license in your possession.

Mushroom Collecting

Salt Point is the only state park in the area and one of the few in California presently open to mushroom collecting. You must obtain a permit and pay a nominal fee. For current information, call the Salt Point Ranger Station at 707-847-3221 or the District Headquarters in Duncans Mills, 707-865-2391.

The best time for collecting is in the fall after the first significant rains. You may collect a maximum of 5 pounds per person per day. These must be for your own use and may not be sold. Edible varieties include King and Queen Bolete, various Chanterelles, Coccoli, The Prince, Cauliflower Mushroom, Hedgehog Mushroom, Oyster Mushroom, Candy Caps, Honey Mushroom, Man-on-Horseback, and Shaggy Manes.

Poisonous or edible? If you aren't absolutely sure, consult an expert before eating any mushroom you collect. (Photo by Russ Whitman.)

The park was closed to collecting during the 1990-91 season because of problems caused by a few insensitive collectors. If it is to remain open in the future, collectors must do their part to minimze the impact of their activities. Observe these important rules:

- Avoid disturbing park vegetation. Try to stay on established trails where possible and do not disturb mushrooms you do not intend to collect.
- Do not rake back the ground cover or dig for mushrooms. An intact ground cover is necessary to ensure continued mushroom fruiting. If you do lift the ground cover to pick a mushroom, remember to place it back down.
- Do not litter. This includes unwanted mushrooms and mushroom trimmings. If you pick a mushroom you do not want, stand it back up to decompose naturally.
- Take only your fair share. Nothing will close the park to collectors faster than people carrying off bucketfuls of mushrooms beyond the legal limit. You are allowed five pounds of mushrooms per person per day for your personal use only. You can expect a citation with a stiff fine if you try to take more than this amount.
- Collect only where permitted. Only Salt Point State Park is open to collectors. Collecting is *not* allowed in Kruse Rhododendron State Reserve, Fort Ross State Park, or Stillwater Cove Regional Park. Stay off private land unless you have *written* permission from the landowner to be there.
- Park your car properly. Do not block fire access gates, and pay the day-use fee if you park at Gerstle Cove, Woodside, or Fisk Mill Cove.
- ***Warning!*** There are many poisonous mushrooms in the park. You can die if you eat them. Beginners should always hunt only with an experienced collector. Avoid all mushrooms that even resemble poisonous varieties and be 100 percent certain before eating any of them.

History

The first people to live in the Salt Point region were the Kashaya Pomo Indians. Evidence of their existence can still be found today in the form of refuse piles called *middens*. A midden can be identified because its sterile soil prevents growth of most vegetation. If you come across a midden in your explorations, remember that it is protected by state and federal law, so leave it undisturbed.

After the Russians left Fort Ross, Mexico began issuing land grants along the northern coast. In 1846, Ernest Rufus and Charles Meyer received the lands stretching from Salt Point to Gualala Point. These two German immigrants called their property, naturally, Rancho German. They owned the land only three years before selling to a partnership that divided it into smaller parcels. Samuel Duncan and Joshua Hendy received the portion

The Ocean Cove Store, on Highway 1 just south of the park, is a good place to stop for food and drinks before camping or picnicking. (Photo by Bob Wale.)

that now includes the state park. The two men built a sawmill on the ridge behind Salt Point in 1853. They also leased rights to a San Francisco company to quarry sandstone on their land. Soon, schooners were carrying lumber and stone from Gerstle Cove to the rapidly growing city to the south.

Hendy eventually sold out his interest to Duncan. In 1862, Duncan decided to move his mill south to the present site of Duncan's Landing at Sonoma Coast State Beach. He leased some of his Rancho German land to John Colt Fisk, who settled at Fisk Mill two miles north of Salt Point. Fisk built a sawmill, houses, store, hotel, and post office at this site, and a lumber chute for loading schooners at Fisk Mill Cove.

In 1865, Frederick Helmke bought some of Duncan's land, together with Fisk's mill and village. For a time he ran a successful lumber business, but by 1876 the nearby timber had been logged and Helmke moved on.

Duncan sold the remainder of his Rancho German property to Frederick Funcke and Lewis Gerstle in 1870. The two dreamed of forming a prosperous town that would capitalize on San Francisco's booming need for lumber and stone. They founded their town of Louisville overlooking Gerstle Cove in that year and by 1872 had mapped out a plan showing streets all over the headlands. They constructed a number of buildings, including a store, barn, offices, and butcher shop. Their bustling lumber operation included a horse-drawn railway from Salt Point to Stump Beach. In 1874 they built a two-story hotel, the largest on the Pacific Coast at the time.

Louisville never achieved the grandeur envisioned by its founders. Within 10 years the easily-accessible nearby timber had been logged, and the lumber industry fell into decline. Tanbark peeling, an essential source of tannin for hides, remained important, but the region's chief enterprise shifted toward sheep and cattle raising, as it continues today.

Tourism became popular after World War II, with campers and hunters being attracted to the Sonoma Coast area. The state acquired Salt Point in 1968 to provide a recreation facility for the public. Park boundaries have been expanded several times, and campgrounds, trails, and a visitor center have been constructed. In 1996, the park was visited by over 360,000 people, or nearly 1,000 people each day!

Wildfire of 1993

The park was severely affected by a wildfire started by an illegal campfire in the South Gerstle environmental campground on November 27, 1993. Erratic winds pushed the fire in a northeasterly direction, crossing Highway 1 at various points between Woodside Campground and Stump Beach. The fire was controlled the following day, but not before burning 450 acres and several structures.

Bishop pine seedlings sprout in the wake of the 1993 wildfire.

You can still see considerable evidence of the fire throughout the park. Dead and blackened trees are especially evident along the road to the Gerstle Cove day-use area. The environmental campground was destroyed by the fire and is not yet scheduled to be reopened. The group campground, also severely damaged, is planned to open again in the spring of 1998.

Fires are a natural part of any forest ecosystem, and they have positive as well as negative influences. At Salt Point, for example, the fire burned away years of accumulated organic matter, exposing the underlying mineral soil. This has helped the germination of many types of plants, most notably Bishop pines and coast redwoods. As you look through the burned areas, you'll see an explosion of conifer seedlings growing in the nutrient-rich soil. Several types of mushrooms also thrive on the burnt ground. Please stay on established trails in these areas to avoid disturbing the fragile seedlings and fungi.

Gerstle Cove Area

The Gerstle Cove area includes a campground, day-use areas, visitor's center, marine reserve, and hiking trails. To get there, turn west off Highway 1 at the entrance to Gerstle Cove Campground at milepost 39.90. Pay the entrance fee at the kiosk. The campground is immediately to the left. To reach the the visitor's center and picnic area, drive down the road 0.5 mile and turn left at the sign. The visitor's center is visible on your right 0.2 mile

The visitor's center overlooks the underwater reserve at north end of Gerstle Cove.

down the road. The picnic area is 0.4 mile past the visitor's center. To reach the park's namesake, Salt Point, continue past the visitor's center turnoff to the parking lot at the end of the road.

Gerstle Cove Campground

This campground has 30 sites that accommodate trailers up to 27 feet and motorhomes to 31 feet. Sites are situated around a tree-lined open meadow. The trees on the ocean side were destroyed in the 1993 wildfire, and their burned-out hulks offer little of the seclusion once found here. Sites to the east were spared the worst of the fire and offer more privacy.

Each site has a table and fire pit. Restrooms with flush toilets and running water are conveniently located, but there are no showers. Reservations are are taken through the state park reservation service from March 1 through November 30. Call 1-800-444-7275. Firewood can be purchased from the camp host near the campground entrance.

A group campground on the north side of the access road has been closed since the 1993 wildfire. It is targeted to reopen in the spring of 1998. Check with park rangers for up-to-date information.

Visitor's Center

The small A-frame visitor's center, open weekends 10 am to 4 pm from April through November, directly overlooks the Gerstle Cove Underwater

Reserve. Here you can get your questions answered and buy books and postcards related to the park.

South Gerstle Cove Picnic Area

This picnic area lies at the end of the road past the visitor's center. The pavement stops in a loop with parking spaces at the south side of Gerstle Cove. Just before reaching the loop, you'll see a large pull-out on your right with several picnic tables. Well-maintained cinderblock outhouses sit between the tables and the loop.

Picnic Area Trails. Several short trails branch out from the picnic area across the headlands. An easy trail northwest leads 0.4 mile to overlook the underwater reserve. Another trail leads northeast up the ridge to Highway 1 and Woodside Campground.

A third trail, starting at a locked gate at the southeast corner of the loop, is not indicated on the official park map. It was once the departure point for the now-closed environmental camp. It extends just over half a mile to the park's southern boundary. Soon after passing the gate, you'll see a steep volunteer trail on your right winding down Squaw Creek to the rocky beach. This access is used by abalone divers to enter the cove.

The rocky point on Gerstle Cove's south end marks the site of the wreck of the steamship *Norlina*, which grounded and sank in a heavy fog the night of August 4, 1926. Rangers assure me the bow is still visible at low tide if you know where to look, though I have never spotted it. The ship's boilers are said to be obvious to divers.

Salt Point Day-Use Area

Salt Point was the spot chosen by Frederick Funcke and Lewis Gerstle for their town of Louisville in 1870. Today, the only evidence of this failed venture lies in the scattered sandstone blocks left over from the stone quarry. A large parking area here gives you access to the headlands and the Gerstle Cove Underwater Reserve. This lot includes a cinderblock restroom structure with a fish-cleaning area and outside showers for divers. A road from the parking area leads down almost to the beach, allowing Scuba divers and snorkelers to unload and launch small boats into the cove by hand. You must return your car to the parking lot immediately after unloading your equipment.

A paved, wheelchair-accessible path leads southwest from the parking area, giving you great views of Gerstle Cove and the southern coast. After a few hundred feet the pavement ends but a dirt trail continues on around to the northwestern end of the parking lot. In the late 1800's, this area was the location of a loading chute for schooners anchored in Gerstle Cove. Lumber and sandstone blocks were shipped from here to the city of San Francisco.

Underwater Reserve

The inlet at the north end of Gerstle Cove has been set aside as a reserve within which all marine life is protected. This is an excellent spot to explore the wonders of undersea life. If you intend to dive, be sure you are properly equipped with a wetsuit and float, and follow the rules of dive safety listed on page 15. Abalone divers and other hunters can swim through the reserve so long as they don't break the surface until well outside its boundaries, marked by bright yellow stripes painted on the rocks at each side of the inlet.

You access the underwater reserve from the Salt Point day-use area. If you have a small boat or kayak, you can drive the paved road almost all the way down to the beach, unload your boat, and return your car to the parking lot above.

Gerstle Cove is a good place to observe the immense bull kelp forests that grow off northern California shores. Strands of this massive kelp grow up from deep below the surface, reaching lengths in excess of 100 feet. Each strand ends in a large hollow bulb as much as 6 inches in diameter from which a large number of blades 10 to 12 feet long hang down. You can often find numerous strands washed onto the shore, especially after a storm.

Salt Point Headlands Trail

Sandstone blocks from the old quarry still lie scattered across the headlands.

A trail across the headlands winds along the coast from Salt Point to Stump Beach. It starts at an old dirt road departing from the northwest end of the Salt Point day-use parking lot. After a few hundred feet the road curves left and another road veers right. Follow the left road for a short distance, then join a single-track trail on your right, hugging the shoreline. After 0.3 mile, a short spur trail branches left to the shore, where you will see examples of the honeycomb-shaped sandstone tafoni.

The trail then curves left around a small cove. The large rock outcrop on your right was an old sandstone quarry. You can still see quarried blocks adjacent to the path, identified by

In the right light, Salt Point's natural rock sculptures can resemble the carvings of ancient civilizations.

the lines of drill-holes along their edges.

Cross Warren Creek, which empties into the cove, and continue along the narrow path. Various trails merge and depart as you head northwest. Keep to the left, staying close to the shore. You may spot any number of birds as you hike. Especially elegant are the great blue herons that frequent the area. They normally stand in a compact crouch, but when alarmed will extend their necks and bodies straight up to identify the intruder.

At about 0.7 mile the trail climbs a small saddle between rock outcrops. As you emerge, you see along the shore a broad expanse of intricately sculpted sandstone. You can detour here to explore the fantastic shapes reminescent of sandstone hoodoos in southern Utah. Stay back from the surf, as the sea is unpredictable. Sets of fairly calm waves can be punctuated by an occasional breaker that crashes violently onto the rocks, sending spray 50 feet into the air.

The local Kashaya Pomo Indians once collected salt from this area for their own use and as a trading commodity. The sandstone forms natural catchbasins for sea water, and when the water evaporates the salt is left behind. The Kashaya gathered it and traded for goods such as obsidian from inland tribes. It was this early commercial activity that gave Salt Point its name.

You reach the headlands above Stump Beach at 1.2 miles. Take the old road to descend into the cove here, which has the only sandy beach in the park.

Woodside Area

The Woodside area, with its campground and hiking trails, lies across Highway 1 from Gerstle Cove. Turn east at the entrance road just south of milepost 39.84 and pay the entrance fee at the station. A mobile home on the left serves as park headquarters.

Woodside Campground

The Woodside Campground offers several types of camping experiences. The regular campground consists of 79 sites on two loop roads set in a mixed pine/redwood forest. Restrooms with flush toilets and running water (no showers) are conveniently located, and several sites are disabled accessible. Sites are reasonably secluded, and each has a table and fire ring. Campsites are subject to reservation from March 1 through November 30. Call the state park reservation service at 1-800-444-7275.

A 20-site walk-in campground provides a more private setting for those who want to fully experience the natural environment. Sites are a half-mile walk from the parking area, and you must carry your equipment to your site. No pets are allowed at this campground. A restroom with running water is located nearby. This campground is on the reservation system from April 1 through November 30, and is open weather permitting.

A hiker/biker campground contains 10 sites reserved for individuals without automobiles. Most users are bicyclists on multi-day rides along Highway 1, but occasionally an adventurous backpacker passes through. These sites are not on the reservation system.

Woodside Hiking Trails

Several well-marked trails branch out from Woodside Campground to the shore at the Gerstle Cove Picnic Area. Another trail parallels the highway from the entrance station southwest to the South Trail trailhead. The most interesting hike is Central Trail, which climbs a wooded ridge to the pygmy forest and prairie.

Central Trail through Pygmy Forest.

Central Trail to Pygmy Forest.

From Highway 1, turn into the Woodside Campground entrance and follow the sign to the hike/bike camp. The trailhead lies at the end of a parking lot just behind the park headquarters. Park in one of the large pull-through spaces suitable for motorhomes or vehicles with trailers.

The trail is a well-maintained old logging road. You begin a steady, moderately steep climb through mixed forest of pine, fir, madrone, and redwood. The understory includes manzanita, rhododendron, oxalis, and trillium.

In 0.1 mile you come to a junction. The left road leads to North Trail, your eventual destination, but it is easier to stay on Central Trail awhile longer rather than turning left here. Continue to the right on a steady climb with only an occasional brief relief from the ascent. At about 0.5 mile you come to two water tanks on the left providing water for the park. Immediately past the tanks, turn left on an unmarked road leading to North Trail. You finally get a respite from the climb, as this road is nearly level for most of its 0.2 mile length.

When you reach North Trail, turn right and resume your steady climb. Bay trees dominate the forest now; their leaves cover the steep trail, making for a slippery path. As you curve left, then right again, notice a hollow stump on your right, blackened by campfires of years past, with a log bench next to it. Remember that open fires are now illegal—their disastrous results are only too evident in the forest surrounding Gerstle Cove.

The trail levels and the forest thins when you suddenly arrive at the pygmy forest after hiking 1.1 miles. Notice the rough, sandy soil that forms only a shallow layer over bedrock. This region lies over the San Andreas Fault and has been pulverized by eons of geologic activity. Stunted Bishop pines, redwood, cypress, manzanita, and bay laurel struggle to extract nutrients from the poor soil.

You walk through true pygmy forest for about 0.3 mile. As you transition out, you climb again to reach the highest point of the trail at 900 feet elevation. You then descend back to a junction with Central Trail.

You have several choices at this point. For the shortest hike, turn right and walk down Central Trail, reaching the trailhead after a total hike of 3 miles. Or you can return the way you came for a 3.5 mile hike. Finally, you can turn left and walk 0.4 mile to a large open prairie, then continue on down South Trail toward its trailhead at Highway 1. Just before the trailhead, turn right and follow a footpath back to the campground for a total hike of nearly 5 miles. Another variation of this last route can include a detour at the prairie along a trail that climbs steeply to Seaview Road or, alternatively, to Kruse Ranch Road.

Northern Areas

Stump Beach

The only sandy beach in the park is located at Stump Beach, and what a beach it is! A sheltered cove with bright white sand and aquamarine water reminds you of a tropical inlet (a comparison you'll soon forget when you feel the cold California water). The sheltering effect of the horseshoe-shaped-cove surrounded by high bluffs isolates you from the rough seas, making this a great place for families.

*Stump Beach's protected cove and sandy shores make this
an ideal picnic spot.*

The parking lot, with picnic tables and outhouses, is just off the highway
at milepost 41.20. A paved trail, moderately steep, descends 120 feet to the
beach. Miller Creek empties on its south side. The fine white sand is covered
with the detritus so common to Northern California beaches: bits of driftwood, bull kelp, and an occasional mussel shell.

Fisk Mill Cove

This popular day-use site has two picnic areas with a number of tables. It
is directly off Highway 1 at milepost 42.63. Be sure to pay the entrance fee
when you arrive. The receipt will allow you access into all of the State Park
day use areas for that day.

The northern picnic area is divided into two lots with a number of parking
spaces, including a center section with drive-through spaces for motorhomes
and vehicles with trailers. The picnic tables, each with an elevated iron barbeque grille, are nestled in a stand of pines 100 feet above the sea. There is

*A visitor inspects one of
Stump Beach's sturdy driftwood forts.*

Sentinel Rock is a good spot for seal or whale watching.

also a dual cinderblock restroom with motorhome-style flush toilets. A short path from the center of the first lot connects with Bluff Trail. The path to Sentinel Rock Viewing Platform departs from the end of the second lot.

A smaller parking lot on the south side of the cove ends in a wooded dayuse area with picnic tables, elevated barbeque grilles, and a dual cinderblock restroom. Several trails branch out from the picnic area across the bluffs.

Sentinel Rock

A short trail leaves from the northern end of the Fisk Mill Cove picnic area to a viewing platform at Sentinel Rock. Just after the trailhead you'll cross Bluff Trail heading right, but you bear left and hike through a stand of Bishop pines. The path curves left as it begins to climb. Be very careful here, as poison oak grows profusely right up to the trailside. You climb up several dozen wooden steps to a wooden deck at the top of the rock. A bench built into the railing is a good spot to relax and enjoy a picnic lunch. From here, you look out over the coast in all directions. On a clear day, you can see Salt Point to the south and Horseshoe Point to the north. Harbor seals often haul out on the rocks far below, but you'll need a good pair of binoculars to easily observe them.

Bluff Trail

This trail stretches from the bluffs overlooking Stump Beach all the way to Horseshoe Point, but most people will want to start from either Fisk Mill Cove or nearby Cannon Gulch.

To hike south, drive to Fisk Mill Cove, pay the entrance fee, and park in the first lot to the right (north). A short spur trail leads from here to connect with the main trail. Turn left and proceed through a pine forest. The trail alternates between exposed bluffs and sheltered forest before eventually

Salt Point coastline north of Gerstle Cove.

emerging into open grassland. For the next half mile you have great views of the intricately sculptured coast along with headlands blanketed in colorful wildflowers. You can also easily hike down to Stump Beach if you wish.

You can explore the northern coastline by hiking the trail north from Fisk Mill Cove. (For a shorter hike, you can access Bluff Trail from any of the large pullouts along the highway north of Cannon Gulch. Follow side trails down to the main trail.)

As you hike north, you soon descend into Cannon Gulch. When you climb out the opposite side, you see various side trails meandering along the bluffs. You may wish to explore these before continuing along the main trail across open headlands.

You soon approach a rock outcrop and adjacent stand of Bishop pines on your left. A short side trail here leads to the Fisk family cemetery. Among the several graves on this peaceful bluff is a marble column marking the final resting spot of 42-year-old Andrew Fisk and his 6-month old daughter, Clara Belle, who died within days of each other in 1874. *"Of such is the kingdom of heaven."*

Continuing northwest, you rejoin the dirt road and pass through an old fenceline. You cross a small, wooded gulch where a steep, dangerous spur trail descends to a rocky beach. As you emerge from the gulch into grassland, various trails enter and depart. Stay on the main, well-worn path following the edge of the headlands.

A couple finds romance at a cove along Bluff Trail.

These rusted iron rings were once used to anchor lumber schooners at Fisk Mill Cove.

In another 0.2 mile you bear left toward a rock outcrop marking the north end of Fisk Mill Cove. Head toward a conspicuous wooden post in the distance. As you bear left of the post, you see several old iron rings embedded in the rock. These and the post are remnants of a lumber chute used to load schooners in the mid 1800's. Veer north past the rock outcrop to see a number of weathered wooden beams from the chute lying on the ground.

As you continue along the coastline, notice the geology of the shore. Soft yellow sandstone is being eroded away, leaving behind darker gray concretions. Stay back from the surf here, for even on relatively calm days an occasional rogue wave will crash dangerously over the rocks.

The crossing at Deadman Gulch is a little tricky. There can be running water here even in late summer, so pick your way carefully along the rocks of the gulch. Deadman Gulch should more properly be named Deadmen Gulch, for this treacherous stretch of coastline has claimed the life of more than one careless fisherman. If you really want to fish here, make sure you have a current will and your life insurance is paid up. It also helps to leave the name and phone number of your next-of-kin easily visible in your car.

You soon reach a long, narrow point extending into the sea. A broad trail heading northwest from here quickly climbs 200 feet to reach the highway at milepost 43.66. Or you can continue straight and approach Horseshoe Point before eventually climbing back around to the highway. Unless you have a ride waiting for you, you'll probably prefer to turn back before starting this last climb.

Kruse Rhododendron State Reserve

Kruse Rhododendron State Reserve was donated to the state in 1933 by Edward P. E.Kruse as a memorial to his father, a founder of San Francisco's German Bank. The area was part of a large ranch established by the family in 1880 on which they raised sheep, harvested tanbark, and conducted logging operations.

This 317-acre park is a living example of how vegetation evolves within a forest. The evolution begins when the original forest is cleared either by fire or by logging operations. In this instance, a severe fire swept through the area many years ago.

The first plants to dominate in the cycle are the fast-growing rhododendrons. For a time, their bright pink blossoms blanket the landscape each spring. Eventually, tanoaks rise up and the rhododendrons begin to decline. The evolution continues as conifers emerge to create a forest of mixed evergreens. Finally, the towering coast redwoods grow to dominate the forest. This complete cycle can take 1000 years.

Kruse Rhododendron Reserve is now in the tanoak stage with the rhododendrons beginning to decline. The normal philosophy for a state park would be to let nature take its course, but since the park was established for the express purpose of preserving the rhododendron displays, steps have been taken to slow the plant succession. A project to thin the tanoaks was begun in 1979 and completed in 1981. Three years later, significant increases in the floral displays were already evident.

Facilities

The Reserve is a day-use area only, and there are no picnic facilities. Pit toilets are located near the parking lot, 0.5 mile up Kruse Ranch Road. A short loop trail takes you through excellent rhododendron displays before returning to the parking lot. A longer 2.5-mile loop gives you a chance to explore the entire park. This rustic trail takes you through mixed forests, shaded canyons, and fine rhododendron displays. In several places, wooden footbridges traverse seasonal streams. The best time to visit is in late April and early May, when the rhododendrons are in full bloom. As a general rule, figure that peak displays occur in the two weeks around Mother's Day.

For Further Reading

Wilson, Simone, *Sonoma County, the River of Time*, Windsor Publications, Chatsworth, CA, 1990.

Lorentzen, Bob, *The Hiker's Hip Pocket Guide to Sonoma County*, Bored Feet Publications, Mendocino, CA, 1990.

Edwards, Don, *Making the Most of Sonoma County*, Valley of the Moon Press, Alameda, CA, 1986.

Brown, Vinson, and Douglas Andrews, *The Pomo Indians of California and Their Neighbors*, Naturegraph Publishers, Inc, Happy Camp, CA, 1969.

The Parson Jones Tree is over 1300 years old and is the tallest tree in the park. *(Photo by Russ Whitman.)*

5

Armstrong Redwoods State Reserve

Armstrong Redwoods State Reserve, three miles north of Guerneville, is home to Sonoma County's last major stand of old-growth redwoods. Here, you can gaze in wonder upon giants already ancient when Columbus discovered America—trees that were alive when Mohammed founded Islam 1400 years ago.

Until the last half of the 19th century, such redwood groves—many even more magnificent than Armstrong—were common throughout the Russian River area. Some trees stood nearly 400 feet tall and had been alive since before the dawn of Christianity. Today almost all of these majestic giants, the world's tallest living things, have fallen victim to the lumberjack's saw. Throughout the Pacific Northwest, less than 5 percent of the original old-growth forest is still extant; in Sonoma County, besides Armstrong only a few small privately-owned groves remain.

This 805-acre reserve gives you the rare opportunity to experience the stately grandeur of an ancient forest. To fully appreciate it, you'll have to get out of your car and walk. It isn't hard, for much of the park is level bottom

Fast Facts

Internet home page: http://www.mcn.org/1/rrparks/parks/armsr.htm
Park headquarters: Adjacent to visitor's center at park entrance.
Hours: 8:00 am to one hour after sunset daily.
Phone: 707-869-2015
Visitor's Center: Open 10:00 am to 4:00 pm
Camping:
No camping in this park, but a rustic campground is situated at Bullfrog Pond in adjacent Austin Creek State Recreation Area. Open all year, first-come-first-served. Backcountry campsites also available in Austin Creek. Road to Austin Creek closed to vehicles over 20 feet in length and vehicles with trailers of any size.
Best hiking trails: Pioneer Trail, Discovery Trail, East Ridge Trail, Pool Ridge Trail. Portions of Pioneer Trail and Icicle Tree Trail have been designated as a self-guided nature trail. Be sure to pick up a descriptive trail guide at the visitor's center.

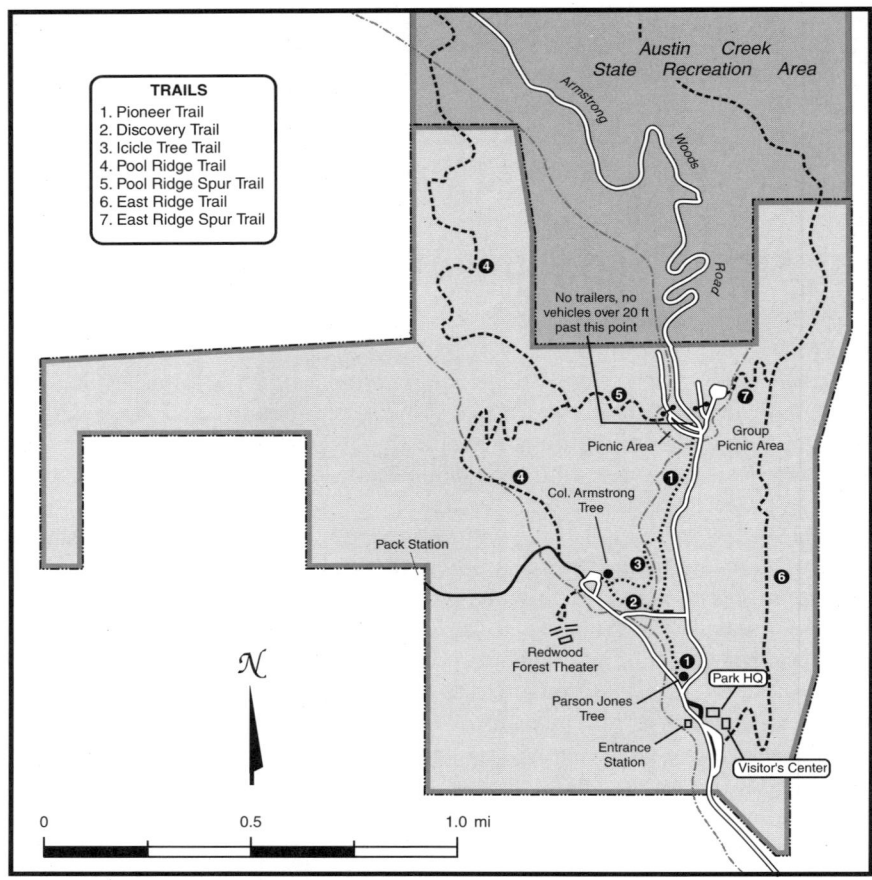

TRAILS
1. Pioneer Trail
2. Discovery Trail
3. Icicle Tree Trail
4. Pool Ridge Trail
5. Pool Ridge Spur Trail
6. East Ridge Trail
7. East Ridge Spur Trail

Armstrong Redwoods State Reserve (above). Park detail (right).

land. Stand in awe of the towering redwoods, then study the complex understory illuminated by softly-filtered sunlight. On the forest floor, notice the ground cover of pervasive, clover-like redwood sorrel. Then turn to the various ferns and wildflowers: trillium, calypso orchid, wild ginger, and fetid adder's tongue. Finally, observe the tanoaks, bay laurels, maples, and Douglas firs that would, if not for the redwoods, dominate the landscape.

Armstrong is ideally suited for exploring the natural environment. Facilities include hiking trails, picnic areas, a large outdoor ampitheater, and a pack station where you can take guided horseback rides. This is also the entrance to Austin Creek State Recreation Area, a largely undeveloped region of hiking and riding trails with panoramic views of the surrounding wilderness. While there is no camping within Armstrong, a 23-site campground is situated above Bullfrog Pond in Austin Creek.

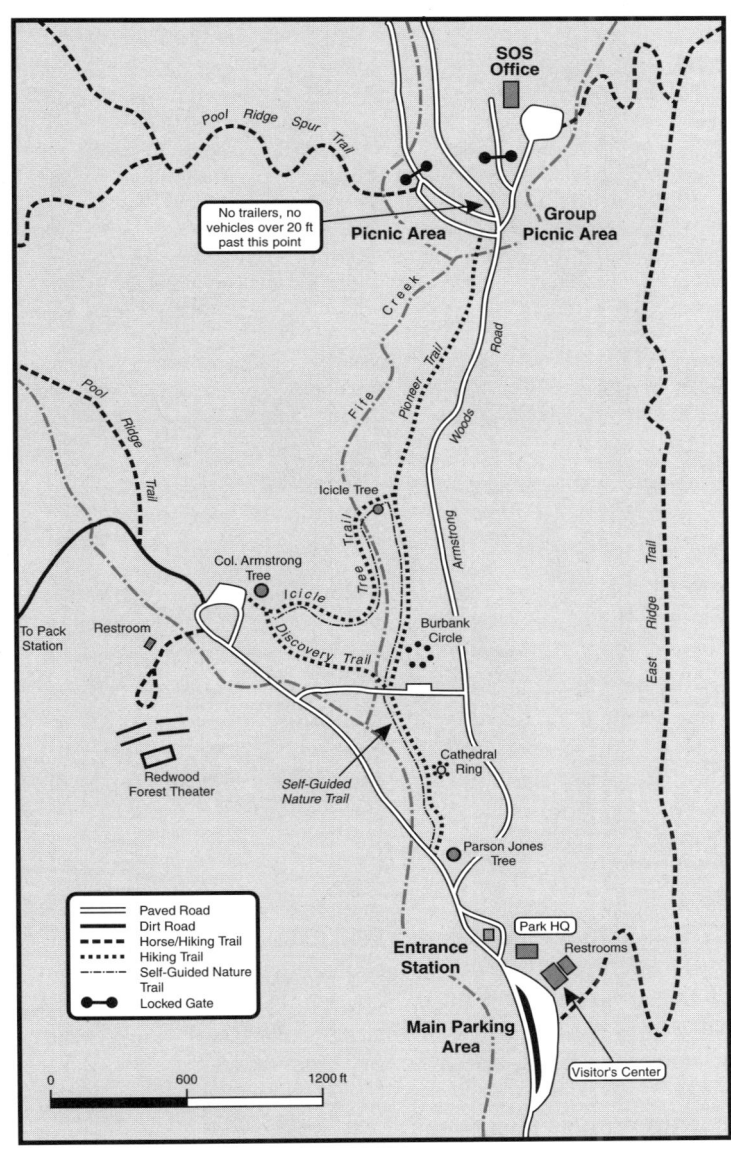

Supplemental Park Rules

The following rules supplement the general rules for California State Parks listed on Page 12.

Day Use Fees. You must pay a day use fee if you drive past the entrance station. You do not need to pay a fee if you park in the main lot adjacent to the visitor's center and walk into the reserve.

Collecting. All living and non-living things are protected within the park and may not be collected. You must obtain a permit from the district superintendent for any exceptions. Geological and archaeological features are also protected. You are not allowed to collect dead and down wood. Fishing is not permitted anywhere in the park.

Horses: You may ride horses on all trails except Pioneer and Discovery Trails. Stay on designated trails at all times. Horse trailers are not permitted beyond the picnic area.

Dogs. Dogs are not permitted on any of the park's trails. Dogs must be kept on a leash at all times.

Vehicles. The maximum speed limit is 15 miles per hour. All park roads are narrow so be prepared for oncoming traffic. Vehicles are permitted only on paved roads.

Mountain Bikes. Mountain bikes are permitted only on paved roads and service roads, not on trails.

Getting There

From Santa Rosa, take Highway 101 to the River Road exit. Turn west and head 15 miles to the Russian River town of Guerneville. With the construction of a new highway bridge in 1997-98, Guerneville finally acquired not only its first, but also its second traffic light. The second light is Armstrong Woods Road. Make a right turn here and drive 3 miles north to the park entrance. The visitor's center and a parking lot are on your right just prior to the entrance station. You can park here for free, or you can pay the entrance fee and drive on into the park.

Natural Environment

The park lies along the drainage of Fife Creek as it descends toward the Russian River. This is a true old-growth redwood forest, with some trees as much as 1400 years old. The towering giants filter out much of the sunlight and keep down the competing vegetation. Lesser trees such as Douglas firs, maples, and bay laurels flourish only at the edges of the forest. Shade-tolerant tanoaks are one of the few species that can thrive under the redwood canopy.

Some of the forest near the park entrance was logged in the late 1800's, so the trees here are second-growth redwoods. Many have sprouted from the roots of the old stumps, forming "fairy rings" of smaller trees around the stumps. These are not new trees, but rather new growths from the old tree.

Redwoods are one of the few conifers that can sprout from existing tree roots as well as from seed. In an old-growth forest such as this, most regeneration occurs from sprouts rather than seeds.

Armstrong's popularity has become a threat to its continued health. Throngs of visitors trample the countryside daily, compacting the soil and destroying the natural ground cover. Redwoods are especially susceptible to this abuse, for despite their enormous height, they do not have a taproot to lend stability. Instead, their shallow root system spreads out just under the surface for as much as 100 feet in all directions. If the root system is damaged, the tree can topple in a strong wind. Redwoods also depend on the forest's thick natural humus layer to retain vital moisture. The effects of a century of heavy use are slowly taking their toll.

The grove's fragile nature was recognized as early as the 1960's. In 1964 its status was changed from State Park to State Reserve. Camping was no longer permitted and visitors were encouraged to remain on established trails. In recent years a series of wooden fences has been erected along the trails to further discourage cross-country travel. As you explore this delicate grove, please stay on established trails and try not to disturb the forest floor.

Early History

California's gold rush in the mid-1800's led to a period of enormous growth in the San Francisco Bay Area. Throughout the region, lumber was urgently needed for new construction, and the vast tracts of redwoods north of the Bay were a primary resource. The Russian River area was at the forefront of this "lumber rush."

In 1860, R. B. Lunsford began a logging operation along the river at a site called "Big Bottom." The surrounding forest was soon mowed down and the village that grew among the stumps became informally known as "Stumptown." Others soon followed Lunsford, and sawmills sprang up all along the river. By 1870, the largest mill was owned by Thomas Heald and George Guerne. Stumptown's residents decided their town needed a more respectable name, and since the town of Healdsburg was already named for Thomas' brother Harmon, they settled on the new name of "Guerneville."

Three miles north of town lay a dense, forested valley. The local Indians called it "The Dark Place" and considered it haunted. Thomas Stone and A. E. Laud, undaunted by the Indians' tales, staked out claims in the densest part of the forest at the site of today's park. The two evidently held the land only as an investment, for they did not cut any timber and soon sold it. The land changed hands several more times before finally being purchased by Col. James B. Armstrong in 1874.

Colonel Armstrong had been born in Ohio on August 20, 1824. Trained as a surveyor, he also served as a newspaper reporter, county treasurer, and

*Colonel James B. Armstrong, 1824-1900. Photo
taken in 1883. (Photo courtesy of Armstrong Redwoods
State Reserve.)*

delegate to the 1860 Republican National Convention before joining the Union Army during the Civil War. Politically well-connected, he was immediately commissioned a Colonel, with a scant 100-day term of enlistment. His commission was more honorary than earned, as he never saw action in the war.

Colonel Armstrong moved his family to California in 1874. With both his wife, Nellie, and daughter, Kate, in poor health, he hoped the California climate would help. (The move didn't help much. Nellie died in 1880 and Kate in 1898.)

A shrewd businessman, Armstrong purchased timber lands throughout the Guerneville area and set up a lumber mill capable of producing 30,000 board-feet per day. He prospered not only in lumber, but also in real estate. As his lands were cleared of trees, he subdivided and sold them. As a close friend of the horticulturist Luther Burbank, he particularly encouraged buyers to plant fruit trees on their lands.

Many people viewed the redwoods as an inexhaustable supply of timber, but Armstrong recognized they wouldn't last forever. In 1891 he proposed that his Guerneville grove be purchased by the state and set aside as a public park. He even donated $100,000 to help the cause. But some skeptics claimed the trees had rotten hearts and he stood to gain more by selling it as a park than by logging it. The proposal bogged down in the legislature. Worn down by a series of financial misfortunes, Armstrong had to give up. He died in 1900.

The fight to save the grove was then picked up by his daughter Lizzie and her husband, the Reverend William Ladd Jones, popularly known as "Parson Jones." The two worked with State Assemblyman Harrison M. LeBaron and State Senator Walter Price. The legislature passed a bill to purchase the grove in 1909, but Governor Gillette was unconvinced. Being an election year, he vetoed what he considered just another spending measure. Parson Jones died the following year. As a memorial, Lizzie named a tree in the park for him, and another for her father.

Lizzie Armstrong Jones, 1850-1924. (Photo courtesy of Armstrong Redwoods State Reserve.)

Lizzie would not give up. Working with Senator Price, she tried again in 1916. This time the plan was to make it a county park rather than trying to convince the entire state. With the help of a committee of dignitaries and hundreds of volunteers, she put together a well-organized campaign. Decorated cars with blaring horns paraded throughout the county. Newspaper editorials were unanimous in support,and when the votes were counted the measure passed by nearly a two-to-one margin. The park remained county property until 1934, when it was acquired by the state as part of the purchase of Sonoma Coast State Beach.

Facilities

Visitor's Center and Parking Area

You'll see the visitor's center adjacent to a large parking area on your right, just before the park's entrance kiosk. It's open from 10 am to 4 pm on weekends and holidays, staffed by State Park volunteers. Here, you can see posters and exhibits that portray the park's history and natural environment. You can also buy a number of relevant books and postcards. Be sure to pick up a copy of the booklet, *Colonel James B. Armstrong and his Redwood Park,* to learn more about park history.

At the parking lot you'll also find restrooms and the ranger station. Both this lot and the visitor's center lie outside the reserve's fee area, but if you do

Armstrong Redwoods visitor's center. (Photo by Russ Whitman.)

park here, consider stopping at the visitor's center and contributing something to the donation box. It's a small price to pay to help keep this magnificent treasure open for future generations to enjoy. If you do decide to drive on into the park, you will need to stop at the kiosk and pay the entrance fee.

Redwood Forest Theater

The historic Redwood Forest Theater lies nestled in a hollow surrounded by towering redwoods. It has an elevated stage and rows of wooden bench seats capable of seating over 1000 people. In earlier days it was used for such events as theatrical performances and weddings. The author and his wife were fortunate enough to be married here in 1976, but it was closed to weddings not long after (the author disavows any connection between the two events). The last major function held here was the Santa Rosa Symphony's benefit concert to help save the grove on August 27, 1995. *Peanuts* cartoonist Charles Shulz and comedian Tommy Smothers, both Sonoma County residents, were among the celebrities to accompany the symphony.

The theater was built during the Great Depression by WPA-affiliated work crews. Construction began in 1934 and the theater was dedicated on Sunday, September 27, 1936. A reported crowd of 3000 people celebrated the dedication that day.

Today, you're likely to have the theater nearly to yourself, especially if you visit on a weekday. On occasion, you may be joined by a family with energetic children or perhaps a solitary figure meditating in silence.

To reach the theater, park in the lot adjacent to the Colonel Armstrong Tree. Walk part way around the loop road to the marked trail heading west. Continue a level 0.1 mile to the theater. There are no picnic tables here, but you can easily spread out among the benches. There is a dual restroom with running water along the path to the theater.

Redwood Forest Theater.

Robert S. Coon Plaque. As you walk the trail toward the theater, look for a bronze plaque on your left, mounted to a rock slab adjacent to an enormous redwood. It honors Robert S. Coon, the park's first caretaker, appointed by the county on July 1, 1917.

Pack Station

The pack station is 0.5 mile beyond the Redwood Forest Theater, on private property at the edge of the park. Take the one-lane dirt road (closed 5 pm to 10 am) and follow the signposts to the camp. This private concession, licensed by the state, offers guided horseback rides for all levels of experience. Advance reservations are required. You can choose from a variety of rides ranging from a two-hour tour to a multi-day pack trip. Guide-owners Jonathan and Laura Ayers conduct the tours, complete with gourmet meals and nature talks. Horse owners can sometimes camp at the pack station and use the corrals overnight. Call 707-887-2939 for more information, or check their Internet web page at http://www.metro.net/ayers.

Picnic Area

The large picnic area is 0.8 mile up Armstrong Woods Road from the entrance station. Picnic sites lie along a loop road branching left from the main road just before it climbs up the canyon into Austin Creek. You'll find tables, barbeque facilities, and restrooms here. At the head of the loop road, adjacent to the restrooms, lies the trailhead for Pool Ridge Spur Trail. This

Coast Redwood
Sequoia sempervirens

Stand a football field on end and you'll get an idea of the height of a typical coast redwood. One tree in the Tall Trees Grove of Redwood National Park is the world's tallest known tree, with a measured height of 367.8 feet. Many others, including the Colonel Armstrong and Parson Jones Trees in Armstrong Redwoods, grow at least 300 feet high. Redwoods live naturally only along a narrow strip of land within 35 miles of the Pacific Ocean from central California to extreme southern Oregon. The temperate climate and lush rainfall along this coast provide ideal growing conditions.

Coast redwoods are slender giants. Trunks of mature trees are typically 10 to 15 feet in diameter, seldom approaching 20 feet. (In contrast, the related giant sequoia, *Sequoiadendron giganteum*, of the Sierra Nevada range rarely grows more than 250 feet high but can reach a diameter in excess of 35 feet.) Coast redwoods don't have a deep taproot to lend stability. Instead, they depend on massive systems of shallow roots stretching as much as 100 feet in all directions. This makes them susceptible to being blown over in high winds.

Redwoods are distinguished by a high tannin content, giving them a characteristic reddish-brown color and acting as a sort of natural preservative. Tannin affords strong protection against insect and fungal infections. More protection comes from the tree's thick, shaggy bark, which insulates it from the ravages of wildfires. As a result, mature redwoods can live as long as 2000 years. Though they don't approach the 5000-year lifespans of the hardy bristlecone pines of California's White Mountains, coast redwoods still rank among the world's oldest living things.

The redwood's branches contain numerous stems covered with narrow, pointed needles one-half to three-quarters of an inch long. Thousands of small seed cones grow from the ends of the stems. It is estimated that fewer than one seed in a million will grow to become a mature tree.

Coast redwoods are one of the few trees that can sprout not only from seeds, but also directly from buds on an existing tree. These buds, called burls, remain dormant until the tree suffers a severe injury such as being blown over by strong winds or cut by loggers. Then, the dormant buds on the surviving stump may be stirred to action. Often, multiple buds sprout simultaneously at several places around the stump perimeter. These new trunks grow around the stump in a circle known as a fairy ring. As you walk through a mature forest such as Armstrong Redwoods you will see that many trees have sprouted from the base of an existing stump.

Until 1944, it was thought there were only two living species of redwoods—the coast redwood and the giant sequoia, both native to California. But in that year, a redwood unlike any other was found in a remote valley in the Szechuan province of central China. From its delicate, feathery needles it was soon identified as a dawn redwood, *Metasequoia glyptostroboides*, a species thought to be extinct for 20 million years. Unlike other living conifers, the dawn redwood is deciduous. It loses its needles in the fall and sprouts new ones the following spring. A sample of this living fossil has been planted next to the headquarters building at Armstrong Redwoods State Reserve.

Picnic area. (Photo by Russ Whitman.)

steep path connects with Pool Ridge Trail after climbing 400 feet in less than half a mile.

An adjacent group picnic area with separate parking can be reserved through the park office. Another large parking lot and picnic area sit just north, adjacent to the Stewards of Slavianka office. The steep spur trail to East Ridge Trail departs from the end of this lot.

Trails and Points of Interest

Several trails run through the park, passing numerous points of interest along the way. Pioneer Trail and Discovery Trail are easy, level walks. Discovery Trail has been specially designed to meet the needs of visually impaired visitors, but can be enjoyed by everyone. Portions of the Pioneer Trail and Icicle Tree Trail have been developed as a self-guided nature trail, with markers and descriptive signs at various points along the way to explain the basics of forest ecology. Be sure to pick up a copy of the descriptive nature trail guide at the visitor's center.

Pool Ridge Trail and East Ridge Trail are more physically challenging. They climb hundreds of feet as they emerge from the forest shadows and continue up the exposed ridges of Austin Creek.

Pioneer Trail

This trail starts at the Parson Jones Tree near the park entrance and continues 0.6 mile north to the picnic area. It roughly parallels Armstrong Woods Road. The first 0.3 mile to the Icicle Tree turnoff also serves as part of the Nature Trail. You climb only fifty feet from the Parson Jones Tree to the picnic area, making this an easy hike through redwood forest.

Parson Jones Tree. Towering 310 feet above the forest floor, Parson Jones is the tallest redwood in the park. It was given its name by Colonel Armstrong's daughter, Lizzie, after she married the Reverend William Ladd Jones in 1901. It is estimated to be nearly 1400 years old. Note the thick vines of poison oak clinging tightly up its trunk.

Cathedral Ring. About 100 feet past the Parson Jones Tree, just to the right of the trail, is a large fairy ring. The trees forming this circle have all sprouted from the roots of a single central tree that fell many generations ago. From the size of this ring it is possible that the current trees represent more than one generation of successive sproutings.

Burbank Circle. This circle of redwoods appears to be an enormous fairy ring far larger than any other known example. Not everyone agrees it is, in fact, a true fairy ring; for no roots from a single large tree can be found. It could be the result of a natural distribution of seed cones, or perhaps even the work of ancient shamans in the tradition of Stonehenge or Easter Island.

Icicle Tree. The large nodules growing on the side of this tree's trunk are redwood burls. These dormant masses of buds can grow into fantastic shapes, stirring the imagination to conjure up visions of strange faces or animals. Although they appear similar to cancer in humans, burls are not harmful to

Icicle Tree (Photo by Russ Whitman.)

the tree. Burls are prized by collectors, who have them crafted into beautiful tables. The long, icicle-shaped burls that once grew from this tree were cut and carried away by vandals, leaving only the less exotic shapes behind.

Discovery Trail

This short trail branches from the Pioneer Trail at the connector road and continues over to the Colonel Armstrong Tree and parking lot. It has several features designed to aid visually impaired persons. A wire cable running the length of the wooden railing helps guide visitors along the trail. Numerous bronze plaques in English and Braille describe trailside features. At one spot along the way, a wooden ramp has been built right up to the side of a tree so that visitors can feel and smell the redwood bark.

Colonel Armstrong Tree. (Photo by Russ Whitman.)

A plaque along the trail recognizes Caroll Smith Knechtle, former supervisor of the Sonoma County Probation Camp. She was a tireless promoter of projects to serve disabled and disadvantaged people, including this trail.

Colonel Armstrong Tree. The most massive tree in the Reserve was named by Lizzie Armstrong Jones after her late father. Although its 308 foot height is two feet shorter than the Parson Jones Tree, it's 14.6 foot diameter is nearly a foot larger. It could be as much as 100 years older than Parson Jones.

Lizzie Armstrong Jones Plaque. Look to the right of the trailhead at the parking lot and you will see an unpretentious bronze plaque mounted on a granite slab. It is dedicated to the memory of the woman whose untiring efforts almost singlehandedly brought the park into being. Lizzie Armstrong Jones died in 1924 at age 74.

Fife Creek. (Photo by Russ Whitman.)

Pool Ridge Trail

This strenuous trail, popular with hikers and equestrians, winds up the west side of the park along a canyon formed by seasonal West Fife Creek. It climbs 400 feet in its first mile and another 600 feet over its final 1.2 miles to a junction with Gilliam Creek Trail in Austin Creek State Recreation Area. Alternatively, you can reach it from a steep spur trail that connects from the picnic area. Only the start of this trail lies within the redwood grove. The remainder extends through a mixed forest of oak, laurel, and fir. Be sure to carry plenty of water and perhaps a snack if you intend to hike any distance along this trail.

To reach the trail, leave your car at the Colonel Armstrong Tree parking lot and walk northwest along the pack station access road. The trail departs on the right after a few hundred feet. Initially, it is fairly level, but after 0.1 mile you begin a steady climb, crossing the streambed (dry except after recent rains) several times. At 0.5 mile you continue your ascent by way of repeated switchbacks up a steep hillside.

The spur from the picnic area joins on the right at 0.9 mile, just as the ascent begins to level. If you're not feeling overly energetic, you may want to descend from here to the picnic area, then along Pioneer Trail and Icicle Tree Trail back to your car. If you decide to continue, the respite is only brief and you soon begin an even steeper ascent for the next 0.2 mile. As the trail again levels, a short loop trail branches left around an abandoned apple orchard. Continuing on, you descend briefly before making a final steady climb for the last 0.7 mile. Finally you reach a spur road from Armstrong Woods Road just west of the Gilliam Creek Trailhead. From here, you can either return the way you came or continue east, joining East Ridge Trail for your descent.

East Ridge Trail

This is the longest trail originating within the park. It stretches 1.8 miles through Armstrong Redwoods and another 2.3 miles in Austin Creek. It climbs a total of 1800 feet over this distance, although only the first 500 feet lie within Armstrong's boundaries. You have several chances for an early return along the way. This trail is suitable for equestrians as well as hikers.

Leave your car in the main parking area just prior to the entrance kiosk. Be sure to carry snacks and plenty of water. You may want to check in at the visitor's center for maps or information on current trail conditions. The trailhead lies just southeast of the visitor's center. It immediately begins a steady climb through redwood forest for the first 0.5 mile.

As you approach the crest of a ridge the trees change to mixed fir, oak, and madrone. You have good views of the surrounding forest as you continue up and down through the wooded hills. You reach a crest at 1 mile, then descend to the junction with East Ridge Spur Trail at 1.2 miles. From here you can either descend to the picnic area and return along Pioneer Trail to the park entrance, or you can continue on into Austin Creek.

If you continue, the trail stays fairly level for 0.2 mile, then rises quickly to a clearing at 1.6 miles. You reach the park boundary and cross a bridge at 1.8 miles, then quickly come to a junction with Meadow Road. This service road connecting to Armstrong Woods Road gives you a second chance for an early return. If you choose to walk down the narrow road back to the picnic area, be extremely cautious of oncoming vehicles.

Continuing up the main trail, you come to Pond Farm's namesake pond at 1.9 miles. Your trail levels briefly, then begins a steady climb all the way to Horse Haven Meadow at 2.7 miles, complete with watering trough a short distance later. You have now climbed nearly 1300 feet from the parking lot far below.

Dedicated masochists may wish to continue the climb another 0.6 mile distance and 300 feet elevation to the junction with McCray Ridge Road. Having traveled a total distance of 3.5 miles it's all downhill from here. If you're still not ready to return you can descend west along the road to the campground at Bullfrog Pond.

For Further Reading

McKenzie, John C., with Stephen W. Hinch, *Colonel James B. Armstrong and his Redwood Park*, Stewards of Slavianka, Duncans Mills, CA, 1995.

Clar, C. Raymond, *Out Of The River Mist*, River Mist Distributors, Palo Alto, CA, 1984.

Lorentzen, Bob, *The Hiker's Hip Pocket Guide to Sonoma County*, Bored Feet Publications, Mendocino, CA, 1990.

Edwards, Don, *Making the Most of Sonoma County*, Valley of the Moon Press, Alameda, CA, 1986.

Sunset from McCray Ridge, Austin Creek State Recreation Area. (Photo by Russ Whitman.)

6

Austin Creek State Recreation Area

The grassy, oak-covered hillsides of Austin Creek State Recreation Area are a far cry from the sheltered redwood forest in nearby Armstrong Redwoods. Austin Creek's 5600 acres offer spectacular wilderness views along 20 miles of undulating trails. Much of the area is accessible only on foot or horseback, and as a result, it is one of the least-visited parks in the region.

Getting There

To get to Austin Creek you must drive through Armstrong Redwoods State Reserve. Take Armstrong Woods Road from Guerneville to the entrance station, pay the fee, and bear right a few hundred feet later. Drive 0.7 mile to the picnic area, then take the narrow, one-lane road that climbs uphill toward the left. Vehicles longer than 20 feet and vehicles with trailers are not permitted on this road. (If you have a motorhome or horse trailer, you should park in the main lot at the entrance to Armstrong Redwoods.)

Fast Facts

Internet home page: http://www.mcn.org/1/rrparks/parks/austinc.htm
Park headquarters: Adjacent to visitor's center at entrance to Armstrong Redwoods State Reserve.
Hours: Day use 8:00 am to one hour after sunset daily.
Phone: 707-869-2015
Visitor's Center: at the entrance to Armstrong Redwoods State Reserve. Open all year, 10:00 am to 4:00 pm.
Camping:
Bullfrog Pond Campground open all year, first-come-first-served. Road closed to vehicles over 20 feet in length and vehicles with trailers of any size. Register at Armstrong Redwoods entrance station. Backcountry campsites for hikers and equestrians are available at Mannings Flat, Tom King, and Gilliam Creek Trail Camps. Register at Armstrong Redwoods entrance station.
Best hiking trails: East Austin Creek Trail, Gilliam Creek Trail, East Ridge Trail.

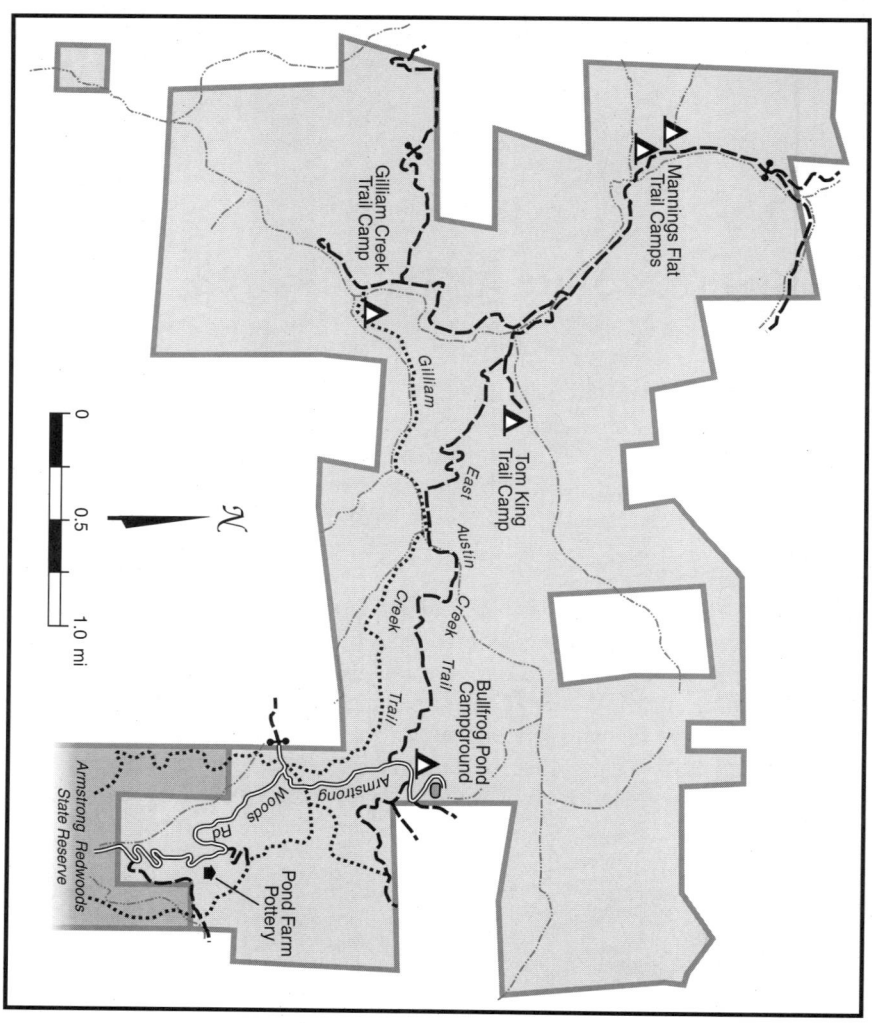

Austin Creek State Recreation Area.

As you climb the canyon you leave the redwood reserve and enter Austin Creek State Recreation Area. This two-way road has several switchbacks with limited visibility, especially for uphill drivers. Take it slow and watch for downhill traffic. If you meet a car coming down at a spot where you can't pass, the downhill car must back up to a safe spot and let the uphill traffic pass.

Sunlight highlights the top of Gilliam Ridge near the old site of Summit School. (Photo by Russ Whitman.)

Natural Environment

The park is a sprawling mass of hills and valleys with few level spots. Live oaks, tanoaks, interior oaks, firs, and madrones cover most of the sloping terrain. Manzanita and scrub oaks grow in the driest regions, while bay laurels, maples, and alders grow in the canyons. In spring and summer, extensive wildflower displays of California poppies, lupines, Indian paintbrushes, shooting stars, and Douglas irises blanket the hillsides.

Some of the animals found in the park include deer, raccoons, skunks, squirrels, and an occasional fox, coyote, or bobcat. In recent years mountain lions have made a comeback, though they are still rare. Black bear have also been sighted on occasion. Feral pigs descended from domestic animals are fairly common in the park.

Waterfall along upper branch of Fife Creek. (Photo by Russ Whitman.)

Birds you'll see in the park include California quail, ravens, black-shouldered kites, wood ducks, and the ubiquitous turkey vulture soaring high overhead. Hawks, great blue herons, and woodpeckers are also common, and on occasion you may encounter a wild turkey as you hike the trails.

Sunfish and black bass can be found in Bullfrog Pond, while trout and salmon live in the streams. With a valid California fishing license you can fish at Bullfrog Pond, but all streams are closed to protect vital spawning habitats.

Austin Creek's climate is hotter and drier than Armstrong Redwoods. While Armstrong is blanketed in sum-

Supplemental Park Rules

The following rules supplement the general rules for California State Parks listed on Page 12.

Camping. Camping is allowed only in designated campsites. There is a developed campground at Bullfrog Pond and hike-in camps at Gilliam Creek, Mannings Flat, and Tom King Trail Camps. All campsites are first-come-first serve. Backcountry permits issued by park staff are mandatory for any of the hike-in camps.

Day Use Fees. You must pay a day use fee if you drive past the Armstrong Redwoods Entrance Station. You do not need to pay a fee if you park in the main lot adjacent to the visitor's center and walk into the park along any of the hiking trails.

Collecting. All living and non-living things are protected within the park and may not be collected. You must obtain a permit from the district superintendent for any exceptions. Geological and archaeological features are also protected. You are not allowed to collect dead and down wood.

Fishing. You may fish in Bullfrog Pond with a valid California fishing license. Fishing is not permitted in any of the park's streams.

Horses: You may ride horses on all trails in Austin Creek. Stay on designated trails at all times. Horse trailers are not permitted beyond the Armstrong Redwoods picnic area, and horses are not permitted on Pioneer or Discovery Trails in Armstrong Redwoods.

Dogs. Dogs must be kept on a leash during the day and in a tent or vehicle at night. Dogs are not permitted on any of the park's trails.

Vehicles. The maximum speed limit is 15 miles per hour. All park roads are narrow so be prepared for oncoming traffic. Vehicles are permitted only on paved roads.

Mountain Bikes. Mountain bikes are permitted only on paved roads and service roads, not on trails.

---

mer fog, Austin Creek's ridges often remain exposed to the sun. Summer temperatures commonly exceed 100 degrees F, while winter nights sometimes drop below freezing. Winter storms have been known to leave a dusting of snow on the hills.

History

No Native American villages are known to have existed within the present park boundaries, though the land was almost certainly used for hunting, fishing, and acorn gathering. Early white settlers also tended to avoid the rolling hillsides in favor of more easily cultivated lands in the valleys below. There are, however, remnants of several early homesteads in the form of old orchards, gardens, and a few houses or foundations scattered around the park. Some of the newer houses now serve as residences for park staff.

The first major development occurred in the late 1800's when a magnesite mine was established northwest of the park at Red Slide. To get the ore to Guerneville a county road was built for mule teams and wagons. Originally known as Magnesite Road and Panorama Grade, parts of this road now form East Austin Creek Trail. Vehicular traffic is no longer permitted, though mountain bikes are allowed.

The mule teams were eventually replaced by a 2-foot gauge railroad that followed the west side of East Austin Creek. The mine closed in the 1920's and the tracks were removed about 10 years later. Though time has reclaimed much of the old railroad grade, you can still see traces of it in spots, including an occasional timber from an old trestle.

A one-room schoolhouse, Summit School, once stood on Gilliam Ridge at a parking area about halfway between the trailheads for Gilliam Creek Trail and East Austin Creek Trail. The exact site of the school is no longer known. Even a group of alumni who gathered for a reunion some years ago couldn't agree on the location.

In 1939, architect Gordon Herr and his wife, the writer Jane Herr, bought 160 acres of the Walker Ranch just north of Armstrong Redwoods. Longtime patrons of the arts, they christened their ranch "Pond Farm" and founded what became a world-reknown artistic community. Bauhaus-trained potter Marguerite Wildenhain came in 1942 to escape Nazi persecution. Her husband Franz, conscripted by the Wehrmacht, joined her in 1947. Others who came over the years included sculptress Claire Falkenstein, weaver Trude Guermonprez, metalworkers Viktor Ries and Harry Dixon, and frescoists Lucienne Bloch and Stephen Pope Dimitroff.

Summers were spent teaching aspiring artists. Students flocked from around the world to learn from the masters. As described in the school's course catalog, "Pond Farm is a place where craftsmen live. Working individually but with the same basic concept as to professional and artistic standards, they have formed a group—the Pond Farm Workshops. The school offers students the opportunity to serve an apprenticeship under the artists of this group." Many courses were taught at the Hexagon House near the entrance to Armstrong Redwoods. (The unique building, designed and built by Gordon Herr in 1948, was destroyed by fire in 1991.) Years later, Pond

For many years this barn at Pond Farm was the studio for acclaimed potter Marguerite Wildenhain. It is now closed to the public.

Bullfrog Pond. (Photo by Russ Whitman.)

Farm was recognized as the beginning of the art movement in the San Francisco Bay Area.

The Herrs found it difficult to keep the strong personalities of the artists in check. Constant bickering wore everyone down, and when Jane died of cancer in 1952, Gordon lost interest in the project. The group quickly dispersed, with only potter Marguerite Wildenhain remaining. She lived at Pond Farm until her death in 1985. She continued to teach and throw pots at the farm well into her 80's. Her house and barn, closed to the public, remain along Armstrong Woods Road.

Much of what is now park land was purchased by developers who envisioned damming East Austin Creek and creating an exclusive subdivision. When this proved infeasible the land was sold to Santa Rosa-based Lumbermen's Leasing Corporation, whose development plans were also thwarted. The corporation then proposed selling the land to the state as a wilderness park. The deal included a plan to acquire adjoining parcels by eminent domain from landowners who were not informed until after the legislation was passed. The

Pond Farm's namesake pond lies in the clearing in this view from Armstrong Woods Road. (Photo by Russ Whitman.)

4000 acres owned by Lumbermen's Leasing Corp. was purchased in 1964, but the remaining parcels took several more years and a series of court actions to acquire. As part of the agreement to purchase Marguerite Wildenhain's property she was allowed to live on the site for the remainder of her life.

Facilities

Bullfrog Pond Campground

Older maps show the reservoir here as "Redwood Lake." It was formed by an earthen dam built by an early settler. The campground consists of 23 sites in a wooded setting on the hill above the pond. A camp host is on duty much of the year. Sites are available year-round on a first-come, first-serve basis. Register at the Armstrong Redwoods entrance station.

Each site has a table, food locker, and fire ring. Flush toilets and potable water are also provided, but there are no showers. Keep your food either in the lockers or in your vehicle to prevent raccoons from enjoying a nocturnal feast.

You may fish in Bullfrog Pond if you have a valid California fishing license. Remember that fishing is not permitted in streams within the park. The secluded setting, far from city lights, also makes this an ideal spot for stargazing on clear nights.

Backcountry Camps

Hikers and horseback riders may wish to camp at any of three backcountry camps. Campers must obtain a backcountry permit and pay a fee at the Armstrong Redwoods entrance station. Be warned that the camps lie 3-4 miles from their trailheads along hikes that descend 1000 to 1500 feet. The return trip is much more exhausting than the outbound hike.

Even if you don't plan to stay overnight carry plenty of water and snacks, and think twice about venturing out during the heat of summer. Always check at the ranger station to learn about any trail closures or fire danger before starting out. Ground fires are prohibited during periods of extreme fire danger. You should also keep a watchful eye out for rattlesnakes along the trail at any time of year.

Gilliam Creek Camp. This small camp is adjacent to Gilliam Creek in a shaded setting 3.7 miles from the trailhead. There are 3 picnic tables, 2 fire rings, an outhouse, and a trash can. The only water comes from the creek; before drinking it you must either use a microfilter or treat it by boiling or by using iodine tablets.

You can reach the camp by hiking along Gilliam Creek Trail all the way from its trailhead or by hiking along East Austin Creek Trail and crossing over a short connector trail at the Gilliam Creek Bridge. The latter route is 0.5 mile shorter but is steeper and more exposed. The last part of Gilliam Creek Trail includes numerous fords of the year-round creek. These are not usually a problem in summer or fall, but after winter or spring rains, the rushing waters may make the camp inaccessible.

Tom King Camp. At 3.1 miles from the trailhead, this is the closest of the three backcountry camps. It lies in a shaded area along Thompson Creek, down a short spur trail from East Austin Creek Trail. Facilities include two picnic tables, fire rings, and an outhouse. If you don't bring your own water you must treat the creek water either by microfiltration, by boiling, or with iodine tablets.

Begin your hike by parking at the overlook parking lot just past the East Austin Creek trailhead. Hike down the trail 2.8 miles to the spur trail on your right. The camp lies 0.3 mile up the spur trail.

Mannings Flat Camp. This site lies along the old magnesite railroad, 4.1 miles from the East Austin Creek Trailhead. You can still see sections of the railroad grade and remnants of a trestle south of the camp. Two campsites lie along the creek in the shade of trees adjacent to a large meadow. Another two sites lie in a grove of oak and fir trees 0.1 mile farther down the trail. Each area has 2 picnic tables with food lockers, fire rings, a trash can, horse hitching rails, and an outhouse. Bring your own water or be prepared to treat the creek water before drinking. Use the lockers to protect your food from raccoons or an occasional wild pig foraging through the camp.

Picnic tables at Mannings Flat Trail Camp. (Photo by Russ Whitman)

Follow the directions for Tom King Camp, but instead of turning right at the junction, continue along East Austin Creek Trail. The last mile of the hike after crossing Thompson Creek Bridge is fairly level. You must ford East Austin Creek just before reaching the camp.

Trails and Points of Interest

Austin Creek is a hiker's and equestrian's paradise. Two dozen miles of trails give you views of forested glades and grand vistas. Spring is especially

Until the 1960's, much of the current park was private property held by ranchers and small landowners. You can still see ruins of old homes scattered throughout the park. Here, Joyce Bacci (center) shows a group of hikers the remains the house she lived in for 15 years until 1967.

inviting, with brimming creeks and lush green hills covered with wildflowers. Temperatures are still mild, unlike the hundred-plus degree temperatures at the height of summer.

Regardless of what time of year you venture out, carry plenty of water or be prepared to purify the water you find in streams. Remember that Gilliam Creek Trail and East Austin Creek Trail both descend sharply for the first couple of miles, so allow three times as long for your return trip as for your hike out.

Besides the two trails described below, both Pool Ridge Trail and East Ridge Trail extend into Austin Creek. Refer to their trail descriptions in the previous chapter. Park boundaries are regularly enlarged, so check with park rangers for additional hiking and riding opportunities.

Mountain bikes are permitted on paved roads and on service roads as shown on the map. They are not permitted on single-track trails. Check with rangers for current regulations before you ride.

Gilliam Creek Trail

This trail leads to Gilliam Creek Camp, one of the three backcountry camps in the park. You don't actually reach the namesake creek until over two miles into the hike. The early part of the trail descends along seasonal Schoolhouse Creek, joining Gilliam Creek for the final 1.6 miles to the camp.

The trail begins 1.7 miles from the park entrance and about 0.8 mile past Pond Farm, at a signed junction along Armstrong Woods Road. There is a small parking area at the trailhead.

The trail leads north from the parking lot, descending through a mixed forest of oak, bay laurel, madrone, and Douglas fir. At 0.3 mile you begin to climb Gilliam Ridge with excellent views of the surrounding countryside. You reach the highest point of the ridge at 0.7 mile, then begin a steady, steep descent for the next 1.5 miles. At several spots along the way you cross seasonal tributaries to Schoolhouse Creek. Look to the northwest as you hike. The reddish-colored vertical canyon on the distant ridge is Red Slide, site of the now-closed magnesite mine.

Your descent slackens as you ford and follow Schoolhouse Creek at about 1.7 miles. At most times of the year the dry creekbed makes for an easy ford. The creek is on your right, not always visible, as you continue to its confluence with perennial Gilliam Creek at 2.2 miles. (If you're looking for a shorter hike, you may want to make a right turn here and follow the short connector trail to return along East Austin Creek Trail.)

Proceeding along Gilliam Creek, the descent becomes more gradual. You cross the creek a total of nine times over the next mile. In winter and spring, you will most probably get wet during these fords, and if the water is too high, you may not be able to cross at all. At 3.7 miles, a short trail on your left leads to Gilliam Creek Camp in a clearing beside the creek.

Just past the camp, the trail wet-fords East Austin Creek, then ends in a junction with the old Magnesite Road. If you don't want to retrace your steps you can turn right and continue 1.3 miles to a junction with East Austin Creek Trail. Turn right here to return to Armstrong Woods Road, 3.4 miles away and 1100 feet higher. To return to your car you must hike another 0.6 mile down Armstrong Woods Road, making for a 9-mile total hike.

East Austin Creek Trail

Purists like to call this trail by its original name, Panorama Grade. Mule teams used to haul magnesite ore along this old county road from Red Slide to the railroad depot in Guerneville. When the 2-foot gauge magnesite railroad was built in the early 1900's the route was changed so the ore cars went to Magnesia Station south of Cazadero. Here the ore was loaded onto narrow-gauge cars of the North Pacific Coast Railroad. Today the trail serves as the principal access route for Tom King Camp and Mannings Flat Camp, two of the three backcountry camps.

The trail starts at a marked gate off Armstrong Woods Road 1.4 miles past Pond Farm. You immediately begin a steady, steep descent along the road. The grassy, exposed hillside of Gilliam Ridge gives you great views.

At about 0.3 mile a connector trail branches to your right and heads to the Bullfrog Pond campground. You continue the steep descent and come to the connector to Gilliam Creek Trail at 1.5 miles, just before reaching the Gilliam Creek Bridge. The trail levels at this point after descending nearly 1000 feet.

At 1.8 miles you begin an ascent up the side of Morrison Ridge. After climbing 400 feet you begin a final descent of another 500 feet. At 2.8 miles you reach the junction with the trail to Tom King Camp on your right. The camp is 0.3 mile up the spur.

You reach the Thompson Creek Bridge at 3.0 miles. From here, the trail is relatively flat the rest of the way. The junction with Magnesite Road is on your left at 3.4 miles. At 4.0 miles you ford East Austin Creek (expect to get wet) and at 4.1 miles you reach Mannings Flat Camp. The road continues another 0.7 mile to the park boundary. Do not continue onto private land beyond this point. You can either return the way you came or cut across to the shadier Gilliam Creek Trail when you reach the connector trail just past the Gilliam Creek Bridge.

For Further Reading

Lorentzen, Bob, *The Hiker's Hip Pocket Guide to Sonoma County*, Bored Feet Publications, Mendocino, CA, 1990.

Edwards, Don, *Making the Most of Sonoma County*, Valley of the Moon Press, Alameda, CA, 1986.

Common Tidepool Creatures of the Sonoma Coast

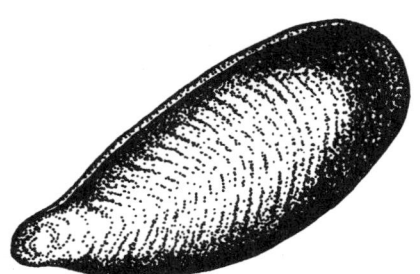

California Mussel

Mytilus californianus

Bluish-black shell to 10" length. Often occurs in dense colonies on rocks exposed to surf, intermixed with barnacles. Mussels serve as food for numerous creatures, including sea stars, crabs, snails, birds, and sea otters. Also a favorite food for man.

Caution: Mussels feed on a plankton from late May through October that causes them to be poisonous. Consult state fishing regulations for more information.

Plate Limpet

Notoacmaea scutum

Oval, cone-shaped, brownish to greenish shell up to 1½" length. Limpets are related to abalones. They have only a single shell, unlike clams, oysters, or mussels. They are found on rocks and in mussel beds between high and low tide lines. They feed on various algae and move only when wetted by waves or when they are under water. Related species include Ribbed Limpet, Rough Limpet, Shield Limpet, Owl Limpet, Dunce Cap Limpet, and Keyhole Limpet.

Red Abalone

Haliotis rufescens

Range from Alaska to central California. Found in rocky intertidal and subtidal areas to depths of as much as 300 feet. Shell to 12" long by 9" wide. Muscular foot can exert a strong grasp on rock, making them difficult to dislodge. Eats marine algae, especially various kelps. Besides man, chief predator is the sea otter. Related Black Abalone is slightly smaller.

Black Katy Chiton

Katharina tunicata

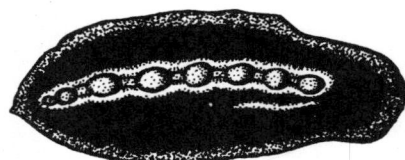

Found on rocks exposed to heavy surf and full sun. Lengths to 5". Chitons are mollusks related to abalone and mussels, and like other mollusks, they eat seaweed. Most species have eight overlapping plates on their backs. On the Black Katy Chiton, the plates are partially covered by a thick black girdle. Related species: Mossy Chiton, Lined Chiton, Rough Chiton, Gumboot

Black Turban Snail

Tegula funebralis

Shell to 1" diameter, dark purple or black with 4 whorls. Ranges between low and high tide zones, feeds on algae. This is the most common snail on Pacific Coast. It can live to be 30 years old. Its shell is a favorite home for hermit crabs. Related species: Brown Turban Snail.

Acorn Barnacle

Balanus glandula

White, volcano-shaped shell ¾" wide. Often found in large colonies. Will attach to rocks, ships, shellfish, whales, etc. Eggs hatch into free-swimming larvae that eventually attach themselves permanently to a host. Barnacles eat plankton they strain from the water. Predators include sea stars, snails, worms, and certain fish and birds. Related species: Thatched Barnacle, Goose Barnacle.

Bull Kelp

Nereocystis leutkeana

The most massive kelp of northern California. Long, rope-like strands to over 100 feet in length grow from deep water. Strand ends in an elongated round air chamber that floats on the water's surface. Numerous flattened blades 10-12 feet long extend from the round bulb, hanging down into the water. After a storm, beaches may be covered with bull kelps torn loose and cast onto the shore. Despite their size, they complete their entire life cycle in a single year.

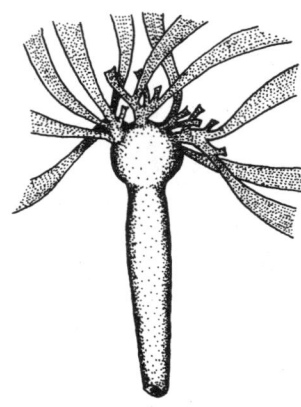

Red Sea Urchin

Strongylocentrotus franciscanus

Spiny oval body to 5" width with abundant spines up to 2½" length. The fragile, shell-like body is formed of calcium carbonate. Spines are used for defense and for trapping algae. The urchin's mouth is a white, bony organ on its underside called Aristotle's Lantern. Urchins are a favorite food of sea otters, as well as sea stars, crabs, and man. Related species include the Green Urchin and Purple Urchin.

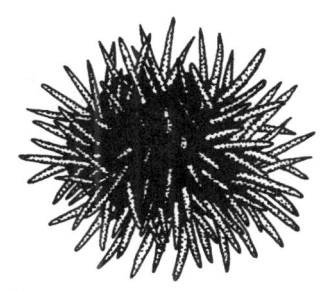

Ochre Star

Piaster ochraceous

Can reach 10" across. Yellow, orange, or reddish-brown body. This is the most common large sea star in tidepools and is often found in mussel beds. Like most sea stars, it can insert its stomach into a tiny gap in a mussel's shell to digest its victim. Sea stars are sometimes called "star fish," but this is incorrect because they are not fish. Related species include the Knobby Star and Leather Star.

Bat Star

Patiria miniata

This small star can reach up to 4" width. It is very common, especially in kelp beds. Color is variable, but commonly reddish-orange. It is found from the low tide zone to waters nearly 1000' deep. Food includes other sea stars, sea squirts, and algae. Related sea stars include species with many arms: Sun Star, Sunflower Star, and Six-Rayed Star.

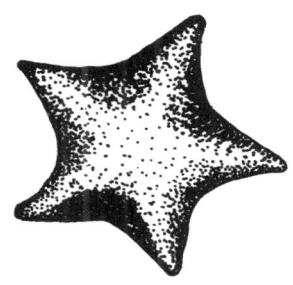

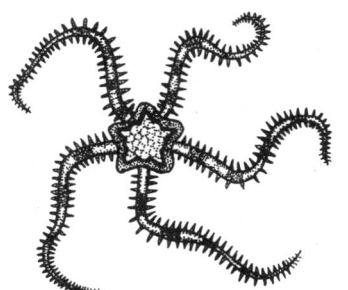

Daisy Brittle Star

Ophiopholis aculeata

Body diameter to ¾" with arms to 3½" length. Various colors, including orange, pink, yellow, white, blue, green, and black. These stars move rapidly when they are exposed by lifting away their rock cover in a tidepool. Several related brittle stars include the Dwarf Brittle Star, Western Spiny Brittle Star, and Burrowing Brittle Star.

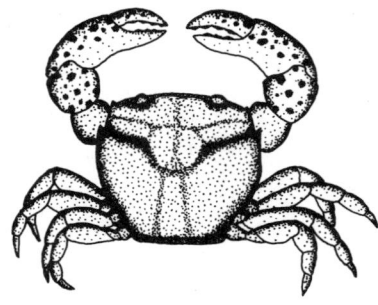

Purple Shore Crab

Hemigrapsus nudus

Deep purple body to 2¼" width, 2" length. Lighter colored pincers have many solid purple or red spots. Lives in rocky shores and seaweed from low to high tide zones. This common crab will quickly retreat into crevices when exposed. Several other species of crabs can be found in the tidal zone, including the Lined Shore Crab, Pacific Rock Crab, and Kelp Crab.

Blue-Banded Hermit Crab

Pagurus samuelis

Body reaches ¾" length, with blue bands on legs and pale blue pincer tips. Hermit crabs prefer shells of the black turban snail, and will frequently exchange a smaller shell for a larger one. These crabs are commonly found in the shallow waters of the mid and high tide zone. The related Grainy Hermit Crab is less tolerant of drying and so prefers the low tide zone.

Sea Sack

Halosaccion glandiforme

Erect, water-filled sacks that can be up to 10" long. Yellowish-brown in color. When squeezed, the sacks emit fine streams of water through several pores.

Sea Palm

Postelsia palmaeformis

Reaches heights to 2 feet. Dark greenish-brown in color. This aptly-named algae is reminiscent of a tropical palm tree. Often found in colonies clinging to rocks washed by strong surf. Best seen at low tide.

Common Marine Mammals of the Sonoma Coast

Pacific Gray Whale

Eschrichtius robustus

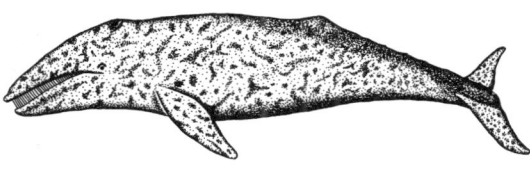

The Pacific gray whale is the most common whale seen off the Sonoma coast. Mature grays reach lengths of 40 to 45 feet and weigh between 17 and 35 tons. For whales, this is on the smaller side—the mighty blue whale, for instance, can reach 100 feet in length and weigh over 130 tons!

All whales are mammals, and they must come to the surface to breathe. Their nostrils, called blowholes, are located on the top of their head. To breathe, the whale normally thrusts only its blowhole above the surface. The spout of water you see when a whale breaks the surface is actually water vapor being expelled from its lungs as it exhales.

There are two types of whales: the *odontocetes*, or toothed whales, and the *mysticetes*, or baleen whales. The gray whale is a baleen whale and therefore has no teeth. Instead, it uses its baleen, a series of closely-spaced plates hanging from the roof of its mouth, as a kind of food strainer. Its primary food consists of amphipods—tiny shrimplike crustaceans that swim in great numbers in Arctic waters. (These amphipods are sometimes called "krill.") The gray whale feeds by rolling onto the sea floor and kicking up sediment containing amphipods. It then swallows a large quantity of this muddy water and forces it back out through the baleen. The mud and water are filtered out, leaving behind the amphipods to be swallowed.

Gray whales migrate annually from the cold Arctic to the warm waters of Baja California. The southern migration begins when the waters turn cold in October. Pregnant females depart first, for they must reach warm water before their calves are born. Next to leave are the non-pregnant females and mature males, followed by the juveniles. Courtship and mating are thought to take place along the migration path in early December. Gray whales tend to be solitary animals, so the migration occurs singly or in small groups, rather than in large herds.

Calves are born in the warm Baja waters the first two weeks in January after a 13-month gestation period. The northern migration begins in early February, starting with the females who became pregnant on the southerly journey. The males are next to leave, with the new mothers and calves bringing up the rear. It is believed that the whales do not feed during the entire migration and can lose one-third of their body weight by the time they return to their Arctic feeding grounds.

When watching for gray whales, it helps to have a vantage point above sea level. In Sonoma County, Bodega Head and Salt Point are two popular spots. You're more likely to be successful on days when the sea is calm and you can easily spot the whale's spout against the darker water. Don't discount overcast days, but windy afternoons when the sea is whipped with whitecaps are nearly hopeless.

The first thing you're likely to see is the spout briefly shooting above the water. This may occur close to shore or as far as several miles out to sea. A gray whale normally takes three to five shallow dives of less than a minute each, followed by a deep dive lasting over five minutes. You may see the whale's back gliding across the water as it takes a breath. Sometimes you'll see it lift its tail flukes above the water as it prepares to take a deep dive. On rare occasions you may even see a breach, where for some unknown reason the whale leaps entirely out of the water.

After being hunted for centuries and driven nearly to the point of extinction, the gray whale is today protected by international law. It is estimated that there are about 17,000 gray whales alive today, nearly back to its original numbers of 15,000 to 30,000 whales—a worldwide population still less than half the number of people living in rural west Sonoma County.

California Sea Lion
Zalophus californianus

The trained seals you see in the circus are actually California sea lions. Males reach lengths of 6.5 to 8 feet and weights from 450 to 650 pounds. Females are much smaller, reaching lengths of 5 to 6.5 feet and weights of 100 to 200 pounds. They have noticeable external ears and their brown fur appears nearly black when wet. They gallop easily on land.

Sea lions are fast swimmers, reaching speeds up to 25 miles per hour. When swimming, they often "porpoise" through the water. They can stay submerged for up to 20 minutes and dive to 400-foot depths. Their diet consists of a variety of fish and mollusks.

Males are very territorial and will bark continuously when defending their territory. Mating occurs in June and July, with pups being born the following June. Sharks and killer whales are major predators. In past years sea lions were hunted for their blubber, but they are now protected by law.

Harbor Seal

Phoca vitulina

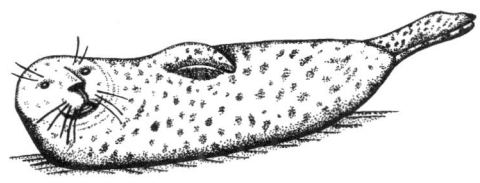

Harbor seals are a common sight along Sonoma County shores, often basking in large groups. They are somewhat smaller than sea lions and are distinguished by their yellow-gray spotted coat and by their lack of visible ears. They move clumsily on land solely by wriggling their bodies. When disturbed they raise their heads, then with an alarm bark they dive into the water. They can remain submerged nearly 30 minutes and reach depths of 300 feet.

The harbor seal's diet consists mostly of fish such as rockfish, herring, cod, mackerel and salmon. They feed at high tide, often swimming up rivers for their catch. As the tide recedes they haul out onto sandy beaches or rocky shores. Fishermen blame them for the large decrease in the salmon catch in recent times, though this is subject to dispute. For many years bounties were paid on harbor seals, but they are now protected by law.

The mating season varies by region, ranging from March to August. Males may breed with several females. They are hunted by killer whales, sharks, and in northern regions, by polar bears. Golden eagles have been known to prey on newborn pups.

Notes

Index

Steve Hinch has lived in Sonoma County since 1974. Born in Seattle, he grew up in the Southern California coastal city of Redondo Beach. Starting at an early age, his avid rockhound parents would pack up the family and head out to various remote desert locations in search of semi-precious stones nearly every weekend. Out of these experiences he developed a dual attraction to the desert and the sea that continues to this day. When he isn't out exploring the countryside or writing books, Steve enjoys photography, swimming, and managing a research and development department for a multinational manufacturer of electronic test equipment.